THE ROYAL HORTICULTURAL SOCIETY
PRACTICAL GUIDES

LOW-MAINTENANCE
GARDENING

ALAN TOOGOOD

A Dorling Kindersley Book

Dorling **DK** Kindersley

LONDON, NEW YORK, SYDNEY, DELHI, PARIS,
MUNICH and JOHANNESBURG
www.dk.com

PROJECT EDITOR Alison Copland
ART EDITOR Ann Thompson

SERIES EDITOR Annelise Evans
SERIES ART EDITOR Ursula Dawson

MANAGING EDITOR Anna Kruger
MANAGING ART EDITOR Lee Griffiths

DTP DESIGNERS Louise Paddick, Louise Waller

PRODUCTION MANAGER Sarah Coltman

First published in Great Britain in 2001 by
Dorling Kindersley Limited
9 Henrietta Street
Covent Garden, London WC2E 8PS

2 4 6 8 10 9 7 5 3

A CIP catalogue for this book is available from the British Library.
ISBN 0 7513 1295 9

Reproduced by Colourscan, Singapore
Printed and bound by Star Standard Industries PTE Ltd, Singapore

see our complete
catalogue at

www.dk.com

CONTENTS

DESIGNING YOUR GARDEN

WHY A LOW-MAINTENANCE GARDEN?

A LOW-MAINTENANCE GARDEN is one that requires only minimal attention throughout the year, and is therefore ideal for people with busy lives, but who also love plants and want an attractive, yet easy-care garden all the year round. "Low-maintenance" usually conjures up images of gardens completely paved or concreted over with just a few plants, but with careful planning and plant selection a beautiful, low-maintenance garden is readily achievable.

REWARDS FOR MINIMUM EFFORT

A low-maintenance garden can have many of the features of a labour-intensive garden, such as family living areas, mixed or shrub borders, collections of special plants, water features, woodland areas, hedges, lawns, and even fruit and vegetables. Plants chosen are those that can be largely left to their own devices, needing little or no pruning, and no staking or tying, and which are relatively untroubled by pests and diseases.

The design of low-maintenance gardens can be exciting and inspirational and is limited only by one's imagination. There is a wealth of fashionable modern materials with which to construct the garden, from gravels, pebbles, and paving, to wooden decking for the "floor". Building materials range from ornamental walling blocks to railway sleepers; and screens and fences made from bamboo or close weave will help to create a stylish garden.

SECRET RETREAT
The design of even the smallest garden can include a secret, intimate area, where you can retreat from the outside world after a busy day. This example successfully combines a number of low-maintenance features – gravel, paving, a water spout, easy-care herbs and foliage plants, and trellis covered with evergreen climbers.

◀ SIT BACK AND ENJOY *A garden full of low-maintenance plants can give you much pleasure.*

SUITING YOUR NEEDS

BEFORE YOU START PLANNING your low-maintenance garden in detail, whether you are starting from scratch or just adapting an existing garden, you will need to assess what you want from it. Do not worry too much at this stage about how labour-saving various features will be, since this will be considered in detail later, but think carefully about your particular needs, because it is both costly and time-consuming to change ideas once the garden has been created.

YOUR LIFESTYLE

First consider how much time you are likely to have available to maintain the garden. It is possible to create a garden that needs only about one hour a week to look after (*see pp.54–55*). You may want, however, to do a bit more in the way of gardening and actually grow and care for plants, perhaps even fruit and vegetables (*see pp.36–37*), which may take several hours each week.

It is very important to take your physical capabilities into account. Elderly and physically disabled people may choose to have raised beds to make plants more accessible; but you do not have to think in terms of maintaining the garden entirely by yourself. Getting help with the gardening can be cost-effective – perhaps use a casual gardener for a few hours a week for any "heavy" maintenance work.

EATING OUT
A "secret" garden room, well screened from the rest of the garden, is an ideal spot for alfresco meals, relaxing, and entertaining. Paving setts make a good hard surface, and are especially attractive when moss has become established between them. The surrounding beds are densely planted with ground-covering perennials that need little attention, and a small tree provides dappled shade during sunny weather.

What is the Garden For?

Consider in detail what the garden is going to be used for, in order to enable you to incorporate suitable features into your plan. Remember to take the whole family into account. If you have children, you will want a safe garden for them to play in (*see pp.48–49*), with suitable surfaces and tough plants that are able to withstand "attacks" from footballs and other toys. Most young children will also appreciate being given their own special play area. If a water feature is to be included, it is essential to make sure it is as safe as possible. Keep pools shallow, and if practical cover the water surface with a sturdy but ornamental grille (*see right*) to prevent accidents.

Adults may well want areas for "outdoor living", where they can simply relax, enjoy alfresco meals, and perhaps also entertain visitors. These will need to be hard areas, constructed with paving, gravel, or decking. It is up to you to decide if you would prefer this to be in a sunny or shady part of the garden. Many people use a patio situated at the back of the house as a living area – but why not be more imaginative and site the patio in another part of the garden, perhaps even screened off with trellis or plants to create a "secret" garden room?

SAFE AND STYLISH
In a family garden, water features must always be safe. This decorative grille over a pond eliminates danger and looks stunning.

How will you and any other members of the family use the garden?

So much for "living" – now you need to consider the extent of your interest in gardening, and plan suitable features accordingly. Busy people who have little interest in gardening may simply want to create attractive views from the house windows. In this case, they are likely to rely on hard landscaping for the basic structure of the garden, and to use carefully chosen plants as "furnishings" to create pleasing pictures for the eye. This is the ultimate in low-maintenance gardening, and once created requires very little attention.

If you have a little more time, however, growing a varied collection of attractive, but low-maintenance plants may be your main interest, in which case you will need a number of beds and borders, each ideally providing different growing conditions. The hard landscaping aspects of the garden can then be played down in favour of cleverly thought-out, easy-care planting schemes.

ANALYSING EXISTING FEATURES

Take a good hard look at your garden and try to decide which features are high-maintenance, and which, if any, are low-maintenance. It is a good idea to save as much as possible of the existing garden, because introducing new features can be very costly, especially if you employ a landscape company to do the work for you. The plans here show a typical high-maintenance plot and provide some ideas on how to turn it into an easy-care garden.

HIGH-MAINTENANCE GARDEN

This garden is surrounded by privet hedges, which require frequent trimming, and has a small lawn needing a lot of care. Mowing is made difficult by the stepping stones, island beds, and overhanging plants. The garden is divided with a trellis screen supporting climbers which need annual pruning. The vegetables and strawberries need constant care and the annual pruning of cordon fruit is quite complex. They may all need pest and disease control. The shrubs and roses must be pruned each year, and the bedding plants in beds and containers replaced twice a year. The pool, containing aquatic plants which should be lifted and divided every few years, and the rock garden, which needs weeding, are both labour-intensive features, as is the herbaceous border, since many plants need deadheading and staking.

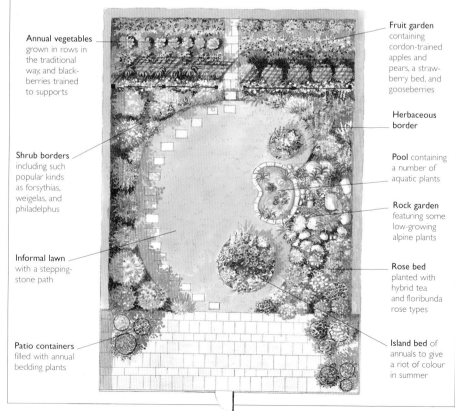

Annual vegetables grown in rows in the traditional way, and blackberries trained to supports

Fruit garden containing cordon-trained apples and pears, a strawberry bed, and gooseberries

Herbaceous border

Shrub borders including such popular kinds as forsythias, weigelas, and philadelphus

Pool containing a number of aquatic plants

Rock garden featuring some low-growing alpine plants

Informal lawn with a stepping-stone path

Rose bed planted with hybrid tea and floribunda rose types

Patio containers filled with annual bedding plants

Island bed of annuals to give a riot of colour in summer

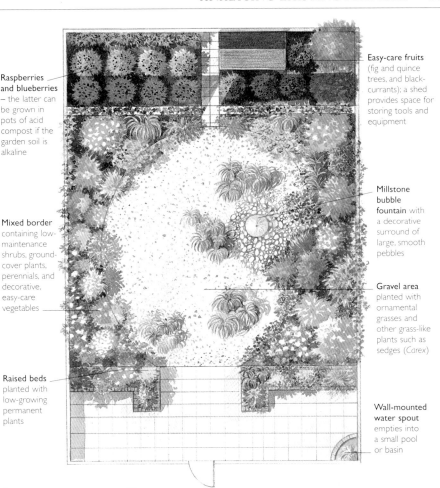

Raspberries and blueberries – the latter can be grown in pots of acid compost if the garden soil is alkaline

Easy-care fruits (fig and quince trees, and black-currants); a shed provides space for storing tools and equipment

Mixed border containing low-maintenance shrubs, ground-cover plants, perennials, and decorative, easy-care vegetables

Millstone bubble fountain with a decorative surround of large, smooth pebbles

Gravel area planted with ornamental grasses and other grass-like plants such as sedges (Carex)

Raised beds planted with low-growing permanent plants

Wall-mounted water spout empties into a small pool or basin

LOW-MAINTENANCE GARDEN

The plan above shows the same garden but with low-maintenance alternatives. The privet hedges have been replaced with fencing, and the trellis screen with pierced concrete-block walls. The lawn has been replaced with a planted gravel area. There are still fruits and vegetables, but ones that need little care. The borders contain shrubs that need no regular pruning, as well as other easy-care plants. The patio containers have been replaced with raised beds of permanent plants, and the island beds of seasonal bedding have been taken away. The water features need minimal attention.

SIMPLE ROUTINE TASKS

• In early spring, cut down the dead stems and foliage of ornamental grasses, and the dead stems of hardy perennials. This neatens the plants and stimulates new growth.
• After harvesting raspberries in summer, cut down the old fruited stems to ground level, and tie in the new ones.
• Remove some of the oldest stems of blackcurrants and blueberries each year during the winter.
• Over the winter, store any pumps used to operate water features in a safe place.
• Cut out dead wood from trees and shrubs as and when necessary.

FLAT SURFACES

When it comes to surfaces that are used for walking on and for outdoor living and play, some radical changes may be necessary. For instance, most gardens have a lawn as a major surface. Lawns are not usually to be recommended for small gardens because they can rapidly become worn and need a large amount of maintenance to keep them looking at their best, including mowing at least once a week in the growing season, as well as feeding and watering.

It may be necessary to replace the lawn with something that requires far less attention, such as gravel or paving. For children's play areas, soft play bark is an alternative to a lawn. A lawn may be an option, nevertheless, for very large gardens where it can actually be turned into a low-maintenance area if you are prepared to give it minimal attention, for example dispensing with both watering and feeding, and mowing far less frequently.

Paved patios and terraces, which are extremely popular for outdoor living, and paved paths, are generally labour-saving; but if the joints between paving slabs, bricks, or setts are not filled with mortar then weeds can become established. If an existing patio does not have mortared joints, it would be advisable to rectify this

Keep work to a minimum with paving, gravel, or wooden decking

situation. Paved areas may also need to be cleaned occasionally with a patio cleaner to remove grime, moss, and algae.

Wooden decking is very popular and relatively low in maintenance requirements, but you will have to give it a little more attention than paving by regularly applying coats of timber preservative or paint. This can be turned to advantage, since it gives you scope for unusual colour schemes.

▲ VERSATILE GRAVEL
Gravel can be used to create surfaces in any shape. A well-prepared site will ensure that you have few weed problems. You can also grow plants in it, such as these ornamental grasses, Festuca glauca.

▶ BRIGHTLY DECKED
Decking needs more looking after than paving, and painted decking requires more regular maintenance than that treated with clear wood preservative, but it can help to create a fashionable-looking garden.

BOUNDARIES AND SCREENS

Radical changes may also be needed for the garden boundary, since it can be one of the most time-consuming features to maintain. Traditionally, hedges were planted around gardens to define the boundary, and many older gardens still have very large mature hedges. Many of these need clipping several times a year because they are fast-growing. Privet (*Ligustrum ovalifolium*) is a good example, and was once very widely planted. If you have such a hedge, replace it with a slower-growing subject that needs clipping only once a year, or with an informal hedge that requires no clipping at all.

Alternatively, perhaps you would prefer to get away from hedges completely. Stone or brick walls are maintenance-free, and you may be lucky enough to inherit them, but they are very expensive to build from scratch, compared with planting a hedge.

Fences are another option, and are now chosen by many people for their garden boundaries. Most fences are more time-consuming to maintain than walls because

HIDING AN EYESORE

Trellis screening a shed supports a pink Clematis montana, *which needs minimum pruning. Low-maintenance shrubs* Mahonia × wagneri *'Undulata' and* Juniperus × pfitzeriana *'Gold Coast' provide further interest.*

they need timber preservation treatment or painting every few years, depending on the type of fence. A few are maintenance-free, such as chain-link fences, which are often erected around new gardens by builders, and chestnut-paling fences.

Internal screens are used to divide the garden and to hide unsightly objects such as sheds and garages. They are also used partially to surround living areas, making these more private. Fairly labour-saving screens can be made from wooden trellis panels, although these need regular timber preservation treatment or painting. If you want to train climbers on them, opt for those that need minimum pruning. As an alternative to trellis, you could use walls made of pierced concrete blocks.

HARD LANDSCAPING

THE MATERIALS USED TO CONSTRUCT the framework of a garden are known as hard landscaping. A wide range is available in garden centres, superstores, and builders' merchants. For many people, making a choice is daunting, and using unsuitable materials can prove to be expensive. When choosing materials for hard surfaces such as patios, terraces, and other living areas, always take into account their ease of maintenance as well as the effect they will create.

PAVING SLABS AND SETTS

These need no annual maintenance, except perhaps giving them the once-over with a patio cleaner, and there will be no problems with weeds if the joints are well mortared.

> ### Setts are ideal for creating imaginative patterns and shapes

Paving slabs are available in natural or reconstituted stone and cast or pressed concrete. Stone is more expensive and comes in subtle, natural colours. Concrete is cheaper and is available in a wide range of colours and textures; it also includes non-slip surfaces. Shapes of slabs include square, rectangular, and hexagonal.

Setts are more expensive than concrete slabs, and are made from concrete or granite; the latter last almost indefinitely. Concrete ones are cheaper, and have a shorter (but still long) life. Setts are usually cube- or brick-shaped, enabling the easy creation of patterns and irregular shapes. They can also be used with paving slabs to create variation, perhaps to edge the area.

PLEASING PATTERNS
In this garden, different kinds of paving setts have been used to create a hard surface which varies in colour, pattern, and texture.

BRICKS AND CONCRETE

A wide range of bricks is available that can be used for paving, but before buying any you must make sure that they are durable, frost-proof, and non-slip. Their cost is on a par with paving setts. They can be laid in various patterns, such as herringbone or stretcher bond (like the bricks in house walls). Patios of various shapes, such as circles, can easily be created with bricks, and they also make very good paths. Try mixing bricks with other paving materials, for example using them to provide an edging for areas that are paved with slabs.

Concrete is a comparatively cheap material for paving, especially where large areas are concerned, but it can also be used for smaller areas, perhaps in combination with other paving materials, such as setts or bricks, to create variation in texture. One great advantage is that it is easy to create complex or unusual shapes with concrete.

Plain concrete can be quite unsightly in a garden, but it looks much better with an exposed-aggregate surface. To achieve this, include an attractive aggregate, pebbles, or gravel such as pea shingle in the concrete mix. Create a fine- or coarse-textured finish by using an appropriate grade of aggregate. A fine texture is better for walking on, and local materials have a pleasing effect.

LAYING SURFACES

- If you hire a contractor to lay a paved area, remember to provide him with a detailed brief of what you require.
- If you intend doing it yourself, consider hiring specialist equipment such as a concrete mixer, a slab cutter, and a plate compacter (for compacting sub-bases).
- To expose the aggregate in concrete, first brush off a thin top layer of the concrete, and then wash off with a spray of water, when the surface has dried for about six hours.

GRAVEL AND PEBBLES

These materials are used to create attractive surfaces, and it is best to buy them from local sources to keep down transport costs. Gravel and pebbles are ideal for using in informally shaped areas. Gravels, such as pea shingle, are both inexpensive and simple to lay. Larger-grade materials, such as pebbles or cobbles, are more expensive, but they are also more decorative.

Gravel can be used either for walking on or just to create a visually pleasing surface. It comes in various grades and colours from rough-textured rock chippings to smooth water-worn dredged shingle, such as pea shingle. A grade between 6 and 12mm (¼–½in), such as pea shingle, is good to walk on, but anything above this will feel uncomfortable. For pleasant walking, the depth should not exceed 2.5cm (1in).

Coarse-grade stone consists of natural stone chippings, and is normally used for creating a decorative effect. Cobbles or pebbles are the most expensive option, and are also usually used for decoration. They consist of rounded, smooth, water-worn stones, in various subtle colours such as

> For eye-catching design, try pebbles or brightly coloured glass gravel

pale grey or pink; diameters range from 50mm (2in) to 250mm (10in). Pebbles or cobbles can be laid loose or set in mortar.

Glass "gravel" and nuggets are two new materials that can add some lively colour to a garden, but are best kept to small areas. The gravel is usually smooth and comes in a range of colours. The nuggets are smooth too, but they are larger, like small pebbles.

▲ RIVER OF PEBBLES
Smooth, water-worn pebbles of different sizes can be used to create some interesting natural-looking effects, such as this "dry river bed".

▶ FORMALITY WITH GRAVEL
A geometric pattern of gravels in different colours and textures, separated by lines of bricks, brings this small garden area to life.

DECKED OUT
Neat and stylish wooden decking creates different levels in this garden. Long-lasting and requiring minimal maintenance (just the occasional treatment with wood preservative or paint), it looks good with a surround of smooth pebbles and associates well with bold-leaved, "architectural" plants such as phormiums and ferns.

OTHER MATERIALS

Wooden decking is very attractive and makes a long-lasting, all-weather surface for outdoor living. It can be raised, or laid at ground level. Tiers of decking will create different levels. Use only timber that has been pressure-treated with preservative. Garden centres and DIY superstores offer special decking timber that is ready for assembly. Tropical hardwoods are very durable and last a lifetime, but are also expensive. Treat decking regularly with wood preservative in natural colours or, if you want more vibrant colour, paint it with yacht decking paint with a non-slip finish.

Decking is also available as ready-made panels or "tiles". These come in a range of patterns and some have a non-slip surface. Tiles are ideal for creating subtle changes of texture, for example with paving slabs.

Raised beds can be built from railway sleepers, bricks, or walling blocks. Sleepers are heavy but long-lasting and cheaper than

POINTS TO REMEMBER

• Any contractor that you may hire to build raised beds will need very careful briefing regarding size and height.
• For walking on, lay gravel on a base of well-compacted hoggin (a finely sifted gravel), not rammed soil, to prevent weed growth.
• Loose gravel needs a restraining edge such as bricks or setts.
• Decking with a non-slip grooved surface is safer in wet conditions.
• Remove algae from decking with a patio cleaning solution and stiff brush.

bricks. Walling blocks and bricks last a lifetime but are the most expensive way of making raised beds. Bricks must be frost- and moisture-resistant. Concrete walling blocks resemble natural stone, and dressed natural-stone blocks are very costly.

"Play bark" is often used for surfacing children's play areas because it is a softer, more giving material than chipped bark.

BOUNDARIES AND DIVISIONS

S OME TYPES OF GARDEN BOUNDARY are much easier to maintain than others. Walls are the ultimate in low-maintenance boundaries, and there is little to choose between walling materials. Fences and internal dividing screens will need regular, but not necessarily frequent, preservation treatment. Hedges can have extremely variable growth rates, and some formal types are very demanding; opting for slow-growing or informal hedging, however, makes them viable.

FENCES AND SCREENS

With wooden fences, in order to ensure a long life, use timber that has been pressure-treated with preservative. Oak and cedar are among the most durable timbers. Woven-panel and close-boarded fences require treatment with coloured wood preservative every 2–3 years. Close-boarded fences have a much longer life than the more flimsy woven panels. Ranch-type, post-and-rail, and picket fences also need regular preservation treatment. Chestnut-paling fences, which have a lifespan of up to 25 years, and plastic-coated chain-link fences, lasting in excess of ten years, are generally maintenance-free.

Screens that are used to divide the garden can be made from wooden trellis panels, but these need regular treatment (every 2–3 years) with wood preservative. Requiring no maintenance are woven-panel screens, such as bamboo, hazel, or willow, but they have a shorter life than wooden trellis. Bamboo is the most durable and also the most expensive. Lasting a lifetime, and needing no maintenance at all, are internal walls made of pierced concrete blocks.

▲ INTERNAL SCREEN
Bamboo panels with diamond windows create a distinctive screen in this garden. Easy-care plants include the box Buxus sempervirens, Photinia × fraseri *'Red Robin', and bamboo* Pseudosasa japonica.

◄ PAINTED TRELLIS
This garden is divided with a screen of painted wooden trellis backed by a clump of bamboo. Although popular, trellis has the disadvantage that it needs to be treated with a wood preservative, or repainted, regularly.

RED BRICK
If your house is built from brick, matching boundary walls will look most attractive. Red bricks also make a handsome backdrop for bold foliage plants such as this Cordyline australis *and* Aralia.

BOUNDARY WALLS

Materials to be used for the construction of boundary walls must be durable and, in cooler climates, frost-resistant. Appearance should also be taken into account since the wall should blend into its surroundings, and of course cost must be considered too.

If opting for a brick wall, choose bricks to match your house. They are available in a wide variety of colours and textures. Bricks must be resistant to moisture as well as frost, to prevent flaking and crumbling. Never use cheaper, less durable bricks because they have a relatively short life and will eventually crumble. Always finish off walls with stone or concrete coping to stop rain from penetrating the wall, since this can cause damage by alternately freezing and thawing during winter.

Ornamental concrete walling blocks with either a red-brick or sandstone finish are recommended. They are also available as dry-stone effect blocks, and these are comparatively inexpensive and a good choice for country gardens. Dressed natural-stone blocks are ideal for those

For ease of maintenance, it is hard to beat an old-fashioned wall

with a deep pocket. Very durable, they are brick-shaped and easy to lay. Reconstituted stone is cheaper – once again the blocks are brick-shaped and simple to use.

Concrete building blocks are one of the cheapest walling materials. You can face a concrete wall with bricks or dressed stone – much cheaper than building the entire wall with bricks or stone. Alternatively, it is possible to add a stucco veneer and paint it a suitable colour with masonry paint.

LOW-MAINTENANCE HEDGES

Hedges can be used either for boundaries or for internal garden divisions or screens, but in a low-maintenance garden hedging plants must be chosen with a great deal of care because some will need much more attention than others. There are two types of hedge: formal and informal.

Formal hedges are trained into a definite shape – for example, the wedge shape is a popular and practical one, with a wide base tapering to about half this width at the top. Formal hedges must be regularly clipped in order to keep them looking neat and at their best. Clipping may be needed once a year for slow-growing hedging plants, or several times a year for quick growers. For a low-maintenance garden, always opt for the former. Clipped hedges are a good choice for formal gardens, especially in urban areas, although they are sometimes used in country gardens, too. There is a choice of evergreen or deciduous subjects.

Informal hedges are the ultimate low-maintenance hedges, since they need no clipping, except perhaps for cutting back the occasional overlong shoot. They look most at home in country and cottage gardens, and it should be borne in mind that they take up much more space than clipped formal hedges, because they can become quite broad. Some shrubs that are used for informal hedges have a very wide, arching habit of growth. Flowering shrubs

> ### In the case of hedges, informality requires much less work

are popular for informal hedges, although there are some evergreen and deciduous foliage shrubs that make good hedges, too.

Boundary hedges should be dense in habit, but fortunately most hedging plants fit this bill. Some gardeners opt for spiny subjects, such as berberis, to deter human and animal intruders from entering.

A FEELING OF PRIVACY
This attractive, formal escallonia hedge is of sufficient height to provide plenty of privacy within the garden, yet it is still easy to clip.

A COLOURFUL BACKDROP
This hedge subtly combines green- and purple-leaved beeches. Although it is deciduous, beech retains its dead leaves during winter.

CLIPPING HEDGES

Hedging plants – mainly trees and shrubs – have extremely variable growth rates. Take this into account when choosing a subject for a formal hedge. Avoid formal hedges that need clipping several times a year, such as privet (*Ligustrum ovalifolium*), box (*Buxus sempervirens*), yew (*Taxus baccata*), Chinese honeysuckle (*Lonicera nitida*), and Leyland cypress (× *Cupressocyparis leylandii*). Opt instead for formal subjects that need clipping only once a year, such as those listed (*see right*).

Clipping is normally carried out in late summer as growth is slowing down (*see pp.64–5*). Do not allow a formal hedge to grow very high since this makes clipping difficult and even more time-consuming. A practical height is 1.5–1.8m (5–6ft). Do not allow the hedge to become too wide, either, because this also makes clipping more

GOOD HEDGING PLANTS

FORMAL
Beech (*Fagus sylvatica*) Deciduous, golden-brown dead leaves retained in winter.
Cherry laurel (*Prunus laurocerasus*) Evergreen.
English holly (*Ilex aquifolium*) Evergreen.
Hornbeam (*Carpinus betulus*) Deciduous, golden-brown dead leaves retained in winter.
Lawson cypress (*Chamaecyparis lawsoniana*) Evergreen.

INFORMAL
Barberry (*Berberis* × *stenophylla*) Evergreen; spiny; bright yellow flowers in spring.
***Elaeagnus pungens* 'Maculata'** Evergreen.
Escallonia Evergreen; white to pink or red flowers in summer.
Tamarisk (*Tamarix tetrandra*) Deciduous; light pink flowers in summer.

difficult. For a tapered formal hedge, a "comfortable" width at the base is 1–1.2m (3–4ft) and about half this width at the top.

Informal hedges do not need any regular clipping or trimming; from time to time just prune back all overgrown or untidy shoots.

PLANTING TO SUIT YOUR SITE

G ARDEN MAINTENANCE WILL BE LIGHTER if your plants are chosen to suit the existing conditions in your garden. It is better to grow a limited number of plants that are likely to perform well than a large range of unsuitable plants that need constant attention to keep them happy. Therefore it is a good idea to study your soil and aspect before planting anything. Most gardens have areas with different conditions, enabling a wide range of plants to be grown successfully.

ANALYSING THE SITE

First look thoroughly at the whole site to assess which areas have moist or dry soil, and which are sunny or shady, or receive sun for just a part of the day. Make a note of varying moisture and light conditions.

Then test the soil for pH – which is a measure of its acidity or alkalinity. On the pH scale, 7.0 is neutral; numbers below that indicate acidity (lime-free conditions) and numbers above it indicate alkaline conditions (the soil contains lime or chalk). On the acid side, the lower the number the more acid the soil, and on the alkaline side the higher the number the more alkaline the soil. Soils can be tested for pH with a simple soil-testing kit which may be obtained from garden centres.

The pH of your soil determines which plants you can grow. For example, there is a range of plants, commonly known as lime-haters, that will grow only in lime-free, or acid, soils. Well-known examples are rhododendrons, camellias, and pieris. If you possess an acid soil, you can specialize in growing such plants. Fortunately, many plants will grow in either acid or alkaline conditions. Some plants are especially suitable for growing in very chalky soils with a high pH; these include Japanese anemones, berberis, ceanothus, clematis, scabious, syringas, verbascums, and viburnums. Again, you can specialize in growing lime-loving plants if you have the right soil conditions. A collection of lime-lovers can be extremely beautiful.

SCENTED HERBS
A collection of culinary and other herbs makes a colourful and fragrant feature in a hot, dry spot in the garden.

SOIL TYPES

- **Clay** – heavy, sticky soil, holding much moisture. Generally alkaline.
- **Sandy** – light soils, with little humus, that dry out rapidly. Generally acid.
- **Chalky** – generally thin soils overlying solid chalk. Alkaline, containing little humus, drying out rapidly. Suitable for many plants, particularly lime-lovers.

PLANTS FOR SUN

Dwarf mountain pine (*Pinus mugo*) Rounded conifer.
Pampas grass (*Cortaderia selloana*) Large grass with creamy plumes of flowers.
Pea tree (*Caragana arborescens*) Spiny shrub with yellow flowers in spring.
Spanish gorse (*Genista hispanica*) Very spiny shrub bearing yellow flowers in early summer.
Sun rose (*Cistus*) Small, evergreen shrubs with white to dark pink summer flowers.
Yucca filamentosa Evergreen shrub with sword-like leaves.

DROUGHT-TOLERANT
Grassy, silver, or fleshy leaves are all good indicators that plants will tolerate drought. They provide an opportunity for imaginative plantings.

HOT, DRY, AND SUNNY

Many herbs are of Mediterranean origin, or come from similar climates with long, hot, dry summers and rainy winters. Therefore, a Mediterranean herb bed would make a good feature for hot, dry conditions, and of course many would be useful, too, for the kitchen. Many culinary herbs are suited to

> Drought-tolerant plants are often highly distinctive

these conditions, such as basil (*Ocimum basilicum*), hyssop (*Hyssopus officinalis*), bay (*Laurus nobilis*), rosemary (*Rosmarinus officinalis*), sage (*Salvia officinalis*), wild marjoram (*Origanum vulgare*), and garden thyme (*Thymus vulgaris*). A number of non-culinary herbs, for example lavender (*Lavandula*), could also be included.

In a warm, frost-free climate, a bed of cacti and other succulents could make an interesting feature. First make up a well-drained bed with specimen rocks, and then choose from the huge range of cacti and succulents available, such as the ever-popular golden barrel cactus (*Echinocactus grusonii*), prickly pear (*Opuntia robusta*), and century plant (*Agave americana*).

There are many other drought-tolerant plants available, including Mediterranean shrubs, bulbs, and perennials, and prairie plants from North America. Many have developed distinctive foliage to help them survive drought. Leaves might be very tiny or non-existent, grassy, needle-like, thick and fleshy, leathery, woolly or hairy, silver, grey, or glaucous. A collection of such plants, arranged in pleasing combinations, will require only minimal care.

In hot, dry conditions, conserve moisture by mulching beds and borders with gravel or stone chippings (*see p.63*).

MOIST AND SHADY

Shady conditions with constantly moist soil provide the means of either creating a woodland garden (*see pp.52–53*) or being slightly less ambitious and growing a small collection of woodland plants. The shade might be dappled, such as that created by trees, which is ideal for growing woodland plants; or it might be unbroken shade, such as that produced by walls or buildings, but this is also suitable for woodland plants.

Another feature that could be created in a moist, shady area of the garden is a "fernery" – a collection of ferns (*see p.53*).

PLANTS FOR MOIST SHADE

Astilbes Perennials with plumes of red or pink flowers in early summer.
Drumstick primrose (*Primula denticulata*) Perennial with mauve or purple spring flowers.
Hellebores Winter- or spring-flowering perennials in a range of colours.
Lesser periwinkle (*Vinca minor*) Trailing ground-cover shrub with blue flowers.
Lily-of-the-valley (*Convallaria majalis*) Perennial with fragrant, white spring flowers.

These plants are now enjoying renewed popularity following a period of neglect after their heyday in Victorian times. Once they have been planted, they need very little attention, and the dead fronds will help to nourish the soil with organic matter.

Very deep shade, producing extremely dark, gloomy conditions, is not really suitable for many plants, and the best thing to do here is to carpet the ground with the few suitable ground-cover plants that are available, such as ivy (*Hedera*).

Most of the plants that like moist, shady conditions will also appreciate soil that contains plenty of decomposed organic matter, or humus; so it is is a good idea to incorporate some composted bark into the soil before planting. Then, after planting, mulch the soil with chipped bark (*see p.63*) to help maintain the cool, moist conditions that these plants enjoy.

LUSH WOODLAND
The ultimate feature for moist shade is a woodland garden where ferns and primulas herald the onset of spring.

CHALLENGING CONDITIONS
A tapestry of tough ground-cover plants, such as these variegated dead nettles, can be created in a shady area with dry soil.

DRY AND SHADY

Shade with dry soil represents the most challenging conditions in which to grow plants. Nevertheless, it is still possible to create some pleasing, low-maintenance

PLANTS FOR DRY SHADE

Bergenias Evergreen perennials with pink flowers in spring.
Butcher's broom (*Ruscus aculeatus*) Evergreen shrub with red berries.
Cyclamen hederifolium Tuberous perennial with pink flowers in autumn.
Dead nettle (*Lamium maculatum* cultivars) Perennials with white or pink summer flowers.
Ivy (*Hedera helix* cultivars) Trailing evergreen.

> ## Choose your plants carefully and prepare the ground well

planting schemes. Dry shade is often found beneath trees, especially large, mature trees, which take a lot of moisture from the soil, and trees that root close to the surface, such as birches (*Betula*). Similar conditions may also be found at the foot of walls that receive little or no sun, and where the rain

may not reach. Suitable plants are mainly the drought-tolerant, ground-cover types, and these can be planted in bold groups to form an attractive tapestry.

It is essential to prepare the soil well before planting by digging in large amounts of bulky organic matter – such as well-rotted manure, composted bark, or garden compost (*see pp.56–57*) – which will help conserve soil moisture. Then, after planting, mulch the soil deeply with chipped bark to help prevent the soil from drying out.

SPECIAL LOW-MAINTENANCE AREAS

THERE MAY BE NO NEED FOR an entire garden to be easy to maintain. For some people, it may be sufficient simply to have one or two special low-maintenance areas, such as the front garden or an area far from the house. You can devote a whole bed to one type of easy-care plant group, such as ground cover or conifers, to create an interesting feature. This is a good way to display a collection of plants, because their textures and colours come into their own.

BORDERS AND ISLAND BEDS

When choosing plants for beds or borders devoted to just one type of plant, it is very important, if the idea is going to work successfully, that all plants are suited to the same conditions in respect of soil and aspect. Even within groups, plants can vary in their requirements. For instance, with ground-cover plants, which are a good choice for low-maintenance beds, there are some plants suited to moist, shady conditions, while others need an open, sunny aspect with very well-drained soil.

First check the entire garden to ascertain what conditions it can provide. Test the soil for pH (*see p.22*), assess its ability to hold moisture or drain freely, and find out whether the site for a proposed bed is in sun, shade, or partial shade. Then decide which plant groups would be suitable, for example ground-cover plants (*see p.28*), conifers (*see p.30*), or grasses (*see p.31*), and prepare the ground accordingly.

Thorough soil preparation is vital for success. It must be completely free from perennial weeds, as these will be impossible to eradicate once the bed has been planted. Dig the bed or border and incorporate some organic matter. This will improve any type of soil. If the bed or border needs better drainage, dig in copious quantities of grit or coarse sand. After preparation, allow the soil to settle for several months before planting (*see also pp.56–57*).

EVERGREEN TAPESTRY
Ivies can create a wonderful texture when they are planted en masse; here the scheme includes the variegated Persian ivy Hedera colchica *'Dentata Variegata' as well as the stiffly upright ivy* H. helix *'Erecta'.*

PLANTING TIPS

• The best time to plant is early spring as the soil is warming up and drying out.

• Plant spacing must be considered. Find out the ultimate spread of each plant, and then plant about one third closer, especially with ground-cover plants and slow growers.

• Planting through a geotextile sheet mulch, such as bonded fibre fleece or woven polypropylene, will prevent weed growth.

• Mulch after planting with a suitable decorative material, such as gravel or chipped bark, laid over the sheet mulch (*see p.63*).

MIRROR IMAGE
A stunning mirror gives the illusion of much greater space in this exciting planting of bold-leaved plants, which includes Japanese fatsia.

BOLD FOLIAGE

Chusan palm
(*Trachycarpus fortunei*)
Grape vine (*Vitis coignetiae*)
Honey bush
(*Melianthus major*)
Japanese angelica tree
(*Aralia elata*)
Japanese fatsia
(*Fatsia japonica*)
New Zealand cabbage palm
(*Cordyline australis*)
New Zealand flax
(*Phormium tenax* cultivars)
Oak-leaved hydrangea
(*Hydrangea quercifolia*)

BAMBOOS
Bamboo (*Sasa palmata*)
Black bamboo
(*Phyllostachys nigra*)
Umbrella bamboo
(*Fargesia murieliae*)

RE-CREATING THE TROPICS

One unusual idea is to plant a selection of hardy plants to create a tropical effect. The best plants to use are those with bold, exotic-looking foliage. Only fully hardy ones should normally be used in a low-

> Bold-foliage plants need no more than the removal of dead leaves

maintenance garden in cooler climates. However, there are two half-hardy ones, the New Zealand cabbage palm and the honey bush, that are worth growing in frost-prone gardens, because they look so dramatic.

These can be grown in pots, overwintered in a conservatory, and then moved outside for the summer. Various groups of plants contain suitable subjects for this style of planting, including trees, shrubs, climbers, and perennials. Generally, they need a sunny site, sheltered from cold, drying winds, which can "scorch" the leaves.

Creating tropical effects is popular in small, enclosed town and city gardens. This is because such plants combine well with architecture and paving. The lush, dense effect they can create also gives the illusion that the garden is larger than it really is, since the whole of it cannot be seen all in one glance. Plants with bold foliage are also a good choice for courtyard gardens or for enclosing a patio or other paved living area.

GROUND-COVER PLANTS

Some exciting, colourful, "woven" effects can be created with beds of low-growing, spreading plants that are grown mainly for their flowers. Unfortunately, in general, ground-cover plants are not used effectively in gardens, and are rarely used as features in their own right. They are often thought of simply as being "convenient" plants to cover ground between shrubs and trees as quickly and cheaply as possible. Yet when a collection is mass planted it can produce some wonderful textures and hues.

Beds of ground-cover plants can be used to make a smooth transition from paved areas to taller and more general plantings, and a bed of such plants in the middle of a large expanse of paving will help to break it up. Borders of ground-cover plants also look good on each side of a driveway, and beds of low-growing flowering plants make a fine alternative to high-maintenance lawns in open-plan front gardens.

It is best to plant ground-cover plants in informal drifts or patches, and to punctuate the planting with taller, more spiky plants (accent plants) such as phormiums, tall grasses, yuccas, or kniphofias. Suitable plants can be chosen from a range of herbaceous and evergreen, prostrate and hummocky shrubs and perennials. For example, for planting a shady or partially shady bed there are many types of ajugas, alchemillas, epimediums, lamiums, hardy

> ## Trimming off dead flowers is an optional maintenance task

geraniums, and pulmonarias; and, for a sunny bed, the choice includes such plants as acaenas, *Anthemis punctata* subsp. *cupaniana*, dwarf campanulas, geraniums, nepetas, *Persicaria affinis*, and cultivars of garden thyme (*Thymus serpyllum*).

COLOURFUL CARPET
This flowering ground-cover scheme includes Lamium maculatum *'Beacon Silver',* Ajuga reptans *'Catlin's Giant', and a hardy geranium.*

CHOICE PLANTS

These ones have attractive foliage, and most flower.

Bugle (*Ajuga reptans*) Variegated cultivars.

Comfrey (*Symphytum* 'Goldsmith')

Golden creeping jenny (*Lysimachia nummularia* 'Aurea')

Lamb's ears (*Stachys byzantina* 'Silver Carpet')

Lilyturf (*Ophiopogon planiscapus* 'Nigrescens')

Pachysandra terminalis

Persian and common ivy (*Hedera colchica, H. helix*) Green/variegated cultivars.

Sage (*Salvia officinalis*) Coloured-leaved cultivars.

Thyme (*Thymus*) Coloured-leaved species and cultivars.

DARING COMBINATION
Black-leaved Ophiopogon planiscapus 'Nigrescens' *teams up well with the golden-variegated comfrey* Symphytum 'Goldsmith'.

FOLIAGE GROUND COVER

Tapestry effects with pleasing textures and colours can also be created with foliage plants, which are used in the same way as flowering subjects. Foliage plants often associate well with paving, and therefore could be specially considered for using in or around patios and other paved areas. A particularly effective feature for a modern garden can be made with a chequerboard effect using paving slabs, or coloured glass "gravel", and squares of prostrate thymes with coloured foliage in which the squares of plants alternate with the squares of paving material. This feature is, of course, more ornamental than practical.

Suitable foliage plants can be chosen from evergreen and herbaceous/deciduous perennials and shrubs with a prostrate or hummocky habit. For example, for a shady or partially shady bed with moisture-retentive soil, you could try ajugas, ivies, and pachysandras, while for sun with well-drained soil a suitable choice could include lysimachias, ophiopogons, sage, stachys, symphytums, and thymes (*see list, above*). Do not be afraid to experiment in your planting, and try some daring or unusual combinations, such as the scheme that is illustrated above. There are many other suitable plants, as a visit to a good garden centre will reveal – most have special areas devoted to ground-cover plants.

As with the flowering plants discussed opposite, little or nothing in the way of maintenance is required. If desired, any unsightly dead flowers can be trimmed off using a pair of shears. If herbaceous plants are used, these will need cutting down in early spring just before growth starts.

A CONIFER BED

Dwarf conifers seem to come in and out of fashion, but there is no denying that they are among the best low-maintenance plants. Once they are well established, they will need no attention. In mass plantings, they create a superb picture with their varied foliage textures, shapes, and subtle colours – all shades of green, grey, blue, and gold.

A bed for dwarf conifers should be situated in an open, sunny position with well-drained, yet moisture-retentive soil. It does not have to be sheltered, since most dwarf conifers will tolerate wind. A conifer bed constitutes a fairly formal feature, and so would be a good choice for a formal garden. To add interest, punctuate areas of prostrate or very low-growing conifers with taller, upright kinds, such as cone-shaped specimens. Space the plants at a distance of two-thirds of their ultimate spread.

There is a huge range of dwarf conifers to choose from. Ground-hugging prostrate or carpeting junipers include: *Juniperus communis* 'Depressa Aurea', spreading to at least 1.5m (5ft); *J. conferta* (shore juniper), spreading to at least 2m (6ft); *J. horizontalis* 'Bar Harbour', spreading to at least 2m (6ft); *J.* × *pfitzeriana* Gold Sovereign, at least 50 by 75cm (20 by 30in); and *J. sabina* 'Tamariscifolia' (savin juniper), spreading to at least 2m (6ft).

Cone- and dome-shaped conifers include: *Abies balsamea* Hudsonia Group (silver fir), 1 by 1.2m (3 by 4ft); *Chamaecyparis lawsoniana* 'Gnome' (Lawson cypress), 30 by 15cm (12 by 6in); *C. thyoides* 'Ericoides' (white cypress), 1 by 1.5m (3 by 5ft); *Juniperus communis* 'Compressa', 45 by 15cm (18 by 6in); and *Picea glauca* var. *albertiana* 'Conica' (white spruce), reaching at least 90 by 45cm (36 by 18in).

TEXTURAL PLANTING
A mass planting of dwarf conifers provides strong texture and subtle colours. This varied collection of popular kinds produces dense cover on a gently sloping bank.

ORNAMENTAL GRASSES

Although these grasses make admirable companions for many other plants, such as shrubs and perennials, they can also create a stunning feature on their own, providing interest all through the year. Unlike many

Grasses move and gently rustle in the wind

other perennials, the dead, bleached stems and foliage of most grasses continue to look good throughout the winter.

An open position in full sun with well-drained soil is ideal for ornamental grasses. A windy site is no problem – the natural habitats of many grasses are windswept, treeless plains: prairie, savannah, and pampas. Site the bed or border either next

GRASS-SCAPE
A combination of dwarf and tall grasses arranged artistically in a border creates a fresh-looking scene in spring.

to, or within, a paved area. Grasses are ideal for gravel areas, too, and they look particularly good in modern gardens. They also go well with architecture. You could opt to have a bed composed entirely of dwarf grasses, of just tall ones, or of mixed sizes. Once established, the only regular maintenance they require is cutting down dead stems and foliage in early spring just before growth commences.

You can select from the different kinds of grasses (*see also p.76*), such as blue oat grass (*Helictotrichon sempervirens*), fescues (*Festuca*), hair grass (*Deschampsia*), Hakonechloa, Holcus, Miscanthus, pampas grass (*Cortaderia selloana*), purple moor grasses (*Molinia*), or reed grasses (*Calamagrostis*).

USING WATER FEATURES

A POOL PLANTED WITH AQUATIC PLANTS is a popular and delightful garden feature, but it requires a great deal of maintenance. Therefore, for a low-maintenance garden, it is necessary to find alternative water features that will demand little attention. This means having no aquatic plants, which may sound dull; if the feature has style, however, this need not be the case. Many of the water features described here are safe enough to include in family gardens.

FOUNTAINS AND SPOUTS

A popular water feature in gardens today is the bubble fountain, in which water is circulated via a hidden underground reservoir to bubble up through a millstone, rock, large pebbles, or other object. This is ideal for informal gardens and where the garden is used by children. For a formal garden, an unplanted pool with a fountain makes a good focal point. Many types of complete fountain kits are available.

Water spouts mounted on a wall above a raised pool or container of water provide more movement and sound than bubble fountains. There are many styles on the market, from the classic lion's head or gargoyle to "designer" spouts. They can also be free-standing, such as a bamboo pipe trickling water into a container or over pebbles. Choose a style to suit the garden. If a pool is not involved, spouts are ideal when there are children in the family.

WATER SPOUT
A simple bamboo spout is a fitting choice of water feature in this Japanese-style garden. The bamboo screen and living bamboos behind and around it continue the theme.

INSTALLATION

• If the pool is to have no aquatic plants it can be sited in a shadier spot than one that will contain plants.

• A pool that has a certain amount of shade will be less troubled by algae, which turns water green.

• The site chosen for a pool must be absolutely level.

• You can construct a pool using either a flexible butyl-rubber pool liner or a pre-formed, rigid liner.

• Fountains and spouts both require an electricity supply. Have this installed by a qualified electrician.

POOLS, STREAMS, AND RILLS

In a formal setting, you should opt for a square, rectangular, or circular pool, either raised or at ground level. Since it will not be planted, install a fountain as the main feature (water plants, in any case, dislike disturbed water). Pools are often included in outdoor living areas, and can be incorporated into paved areas and decking. An unplanted pool

> ### Match the style of the water feature with the style of the garden

does not have to be very deep – shallow water can still create a stunning effect, as dramatically illustrated above.

In an informal garden, the pool can be more irregular in shape, although it is advisable to avoid anything particularly complicated, and is best sited at ground level, or even sunken. It could be placed where it mirrors an eye-catching feature such as a statue or a specimen plant.

▲ STYLISH POOL
This unusual shallow pool has been lined with coloured glass "gravel", laid in a spiral pattern.

◄ BUBBLE FOUNTAIN
Water, circulated via a hidden reservoir, bubbles up through this shapely rock.

Surround it with easy-care, moisture-loving perennials such as astilbes, hemerocallis, and royal fern (*Osmunda regalis*).

A circulating water course joining two or more separate pools is a more ambitious, but, once constructed, still low-maintenance feature, and an imaginative idea for either a sloping garden or one which has various levels. It might be a wide, shallow stream – a good choice for an informal garden – or a rill, which can be a narrow, formal stream, ideal for a formal garden (*see pp.46–47*). The stream or rill could incorporate a small waterfall or two, and be edged with easy-care, moisture-loving perennials.

RAISED BEDS AND CONTAINERS

O FTEN, RAISED BEDS ARE THOUGHT OF only in terms of making gardening easier for elderly or disabled people, and while they can be the perfect solution in that respect they also make attractive features in their own right. They are a good option for low-maintenance gardens compared with most small containers such as patio pots and tubs, but if you really want planted pots there are ways of reducing maintenance, and even unplanted containers look good.

ADVANTAGES OF RAISED BEDS

Because raised beds contain a large volume of soil, they tend to dry out less rapidly than smaller containers such as patio pots and tubs. More imaginative planting schemes are possible, and the right type of soil can be provided for plants irrespective of the soil type in the rest of the garden. Planting and maintenance are also easier for less able-bodied people. Try to make raised beds an integral part of the garden design. They can be a means of creating different levels. Even a low raised border, 30cm (12in) high, might make a sufficient change of level. Raised beds can also be used as terracing on slopes, and they are often placed in and around a patio, perhaps partially enclosing it. A group of, say, three beds, perhaps of different heights and all interlocking, often looks better than single ones dotted around the garden.

Raised beds can be built from brick, natural stone, or ornamental concrete walling blocks. Timber is another suitable

RAISED BEDS

- Raised beds should ideally be sited on a soil base to ensure there will be good drainage within the bed.
- Build brick, stone, and concrete retaining walls on a concrete foundation.
- Lay railway sleepers on a foundation of rammed gravel. Drive metal rods through pre-drilled holes in the sleepers and into the ground for stability.
- Place a layer of hardcore in the base of the bed for improved drainage.
- Fill the raised bed with good-quality topsoil.

CONTAINING THE SLOPE
Sections of railway sleeper, inserted upright, make a substantial raised bed in this garden, and blend in well with the surroundings.

ORNAMENTAL TOUCH
A terracotta urn adds decorative value to this
planting of black bamboo (Phyllostachys nigra)
and blue fescue (Festuca glauca *'Elijah Blue'*).

material, especially in the form of railway
sleepers, which are suitable for creating
large, low beds, which should be no more
than three sleepers high. Log rolls (in which
a series of logs of similar length are wired
closely but flexibly together) can also be

Raised beds should be designed to match the style of the garden

used for low beds, setting them into the
ground for stability, and these are ideal
for creating irregularly shaped beds.

Beds can vary in height. If they are to
be tended from a standing position, 90cm
(36in) is a good height, but this should be
reduced to 60cm (24in) if the gardener will
be sitting. A maximum width of 1.2m (4ft)
is best if there is all-round access, and 60cm
(24in) if access is from one side only.

USING CONTAINERS

Planted garden containers are usually high-
maintenance features because of their need
for frequent watering in warm weather.
Filling them with seasonal bedding plants,
which is extremely popular, is also labour-
intensive. If, however, you really do want
planted containers, then consider using
permanent drought-tolerant plants such as
yuccas, kniphofias, or an ornamental grass
like blue oat-grass (*Helictotrichon semper-*
virens), all of which will survive with less
frequent watering. Remember that glazed
clay pots tend to dry out less quickly than
unglazed ones. After planting, topdress the
compost with glass "gravel", real gravel, or
smooth pebbles to prevent rapid drying out
and to create an attractive finish.

Unplanted decorative containers such
as ornate terracotta urns can considerably
enhance a patio. Empty pots can be placed,
singly or in groups, among plants such as
grasses in a border. Coloured ceramic pots
or rusty metal containers can also be used
to complement or contrast with plants.

PLANTED CONTAINER
Drought-tolerant Yucca gloriosa *'Variegata',*
in a glazed container topdressed with pebbles,
makes a low-maintenance feature on this patio.

THE KITCHEN GARDEN

Y OU NEED NOT GO WITHOUT home-grown vegetables and fruit just because you have a low-maintenance garden. Although it is true that most kinds are highly labour-intensive and therefore completely unsuitable for an easy-care garden, there are a few that will yield good returns for minimal attention. These can either be grown in a special kitchen-garden area, if you have the room, or included in ornamental beds and borders, especially the more decorative ones.

WHICH VEGETABLES?

The more decorative kinds of vegetables are well suited to ornamental beds and borders, where they can be combined with shrubs and hardy perennials. The globe artichoke, a frost-hardy perennial with very attractive, deeply cut foliage, is especially fine for this purpose. Rhubarb, with its large leaves and red stems, also looks good in a shrub border. This, too, is a hardy perennial and needs little attention once planted.

There are several decorative annual vegetables worth considering which need little attention once their seeds have been sown in the spring, apart from thinning

out of the seedlings. Loose-leaf or non-hearting lettuce, with its green or reddish, deeply cut foliage that looks so attractive in a salad, can also be used to make an unusual edging to a bed or border.

Beetroot has eye-catching red foliage that combines well with many ornamental plants in a bed or border. The related chard or leaf beet is a leafy cut-and-come-again vegetable that is available in a number of different cultivars with decorative stems in white, red, and other colours.

Runner beans produce attractive, scarlet, white, or pink flowers, which earns them a place in flower borders. You can train these

GLORIOUS GLOBES
The globe artichoke is as decorative as any hardy perennial. The immature flower heads are used as a gourmet vegetable.

VEGETABLES

- For best results, grow your vegetables in fertile, moisture-retentive soil.
- Choose an open, sunny position for a good crop.
- Sow seeds in spring when the soil is starting to warm up and dry out.
- Sow seeds as thinly as possible in order to avoid too much thinning out of the seedlings later on.
- Water vegetables well if the soil starts drying out.

BEANS IN THE BORDER
Runner beans climbing through a wigwam-shaped support add colour to a mixed border with their profusion of summer flowers.

climbers up a wigwam of bamboo canes, 1.8m (6ft) high, or up one of the cone-shaped willow or hazel plant supports that are usually available from garden centres, which are much more attractive than canes. Alternatively, you could try using a metal obelisk, which will look good in the border even before the beans start to grow up it.

Within the onion family, shallots are by far the easiest to grow. All you need to do is plant the small bulbs or sets in spring, and then wait for them to produce clusters of edible bulbs in late summer. These vegetables are not particularly decorative to look at, and are therefore candidates for growing in a small kitchen-garden area.

WHICH FRUIT?

Several types of fruit trees can be included in the ornamental parts of the garden; these include crab apples – both the culinary and edible ornamental kinds – quince, and the black mulberry. The common fig makes a large, handsome tree with an ultimate spread of 4m (12ft). None of these trees need pruning, except for the removal of any dead or dying branches.

For the kitchen garden, try some soft fruits. Summer-fruiting raspberries need only simple annual pruning: cut down to

> ## Low-maintenance soft fruits can be highly productive in summer

ground level all fruited stems after cropping and then tie in new canes to a system of horizontal wires. Blackcurrants only need the complete removal in winter of up to one-third of stems that are two or more years old. Do not remove one-year-old stems – these are the ones that will produce fruit. Highbush blueberries require a very acid soil; grow them in containers if your soil is neutral or alkaline. Cut out some of the oldest stems each year in winter.

GROWING FRUIT

- Grow in a fertile, moisture-retentive soil, and provide an open, yet sheltered, sunny position to ensure that the fruits ripen well.
- All fruits benefit from an application of general-purpose fertilizer each spring.
- For raspberries, provide a system of posts, about 1.8m (6ft) high, and taut horizontal wires at 75cm (30in), 90cm (36in), and 1.6m (5½ft) to support the stems.
- Water soft fruits well in summer if the soil dries out, as they like a constantly moist soil.
- When pruning, use really sharp secateurs or pruning saw to ensure smooth cuts – these will heal more quickly than ragged wounds.

LOW-MAINTENANCE LAWNS

To LOOK GOOD IN SMALL GARDENS lawns need a great deal of care all year round. They are subjected to a large amount of wear and tear, and will invariably develop unsightly bare patches. For a low-maintenance garden, consider other options, such as gravel or paving. For large gardens, however, a lawn can be a cheap and easy-care option. It does not have to be highly maintained – simply mowing as and when required will be sufficient.

WHY CHOOSE A GRASS LAWN?

In a large garden – that is, one of more than 0.1 hectares (¼ acre) in total area, a grass lawn helps to set off the beds and borders. It also creates an open space in the centre of the garden – which is one of the basic "rules" in garden design. Larger gardens are often informal in style, with a minimum amount of hard landscaping and a sweeping expanse of lawn with gently curving edges and perhaps some wide, meandering grass paths linking it to other parts of the garden. When designing a lawn for a large garden, avoid tightly curving or fussy edges, and do not incorporate too many island beds or trees into the lawn;

either of these will make it both difficult and time-consuming to mow. The lawn should be formed of hard-wearing utility grasses rather than fine ornamental kinds that would need a lot of care and attention and probably decline and die out if not maintained to a high standard.

A large lawn will be relatively easy for you to look after if you adopt a policy of minimum maintenance. Forget all about feeding and watering, and simply mow the grass when necessary – it does not have to be striped or cut extremely short. Always use a suitable large mower: this means either a self-propelled rotary mower or, for really large areas, a ride-on type.

GRASSING OVER
For a large garden, sweeping expanses of grass set off the borders and can be relatively inexpensive to maintain.

WHICH GRASS?

• Use hardwearing utility grasses to create a large lawn that is to receive minimal maintenance. Try to buy a grass-seed mixture that contains primarily perennial ryegrass. Modern cultivars of this grass have finer leaves than older kinds, so will create an attractive surface.

• Avoid grass-seed mixtures designed for fine lawns, which primarily consist of fescue and bent grasses.

CARPETING WITH COLOUR
Creeping thymes (Thymus), *which have aromatic foliage, are an alternative to a grass lawn, and have the added bonus of flowering.*

OTHER OPTIONS

In smaller gardens, as an alternative to grass, lawns can be created with low-growing, spreading, evergreen, aromatic plants (*see pp.74–75*). Such lawns are more decorative than practical, and are unlikely to stand up to a lot of use. They will not object, however, to being walked over occasionally; this releases the scent of plants like thymes, chamomile, and mints.

These lawns can be a feature in a patio or courtyard garden, and make a pleasing surround at the base of a statue, sundial,

---

Grass alternatives are really practical only for small gardens

---

ornamental urn, or raised pond. They also look attractive adjacent to a patio or path where they can be allowed to creep over and "soften" the edges. You could create a lawn with a patchwork effect by using several different types of plant "woven in" together. Very unusual is a waved lawn created with grey- or silver-leaved thymes.

EASY MOWING

- If you do not have time to mow the lawn, get a gardening firm or a jobbing gardener to mow it on a regular basis.
- In spring and summer, a low-maintenance lawn needs mowing once every 7–10 days. It will need occasional mowing during autumn, and none in winter.
- Never be tempted to mow the lawn during prolonged periods of drought in summer when the grass is not growing.

SPRING HIGHLIGHTS
A long-grass area planted with naturalized spring bulbs needs cutting only once a year, once the bulbs have died down completely.

First form the soil into gentle "waves" or undulations, and then plant each wave with a different sort of thyme.

Such non-grass lawns do not require the frequent mowing needed by grass lawns, but they should still be trimmed on a fairly regular basis in order to promote compact-ness of growth and a neat appearance. They can be cut with a nylon-line trimmer or a rotary mower; for very small areas, you can even use hand shears.

Long-grass areas planted with spring bulbs, with regularly mown paths running through them, are very low-maintenance (*see pp.54–55*). The long-grass areas need cutting only once a year, in mid- to late summer, once the bulbs have died down.

SEASONAL CHANGES

A GARDEN IS THERE TO BE ENJOYED all the year round, not just in summer, so take this into account when you are designing and planting it. Make sure that mixed beds and borders contain plants to provide interest and colour for all four seasons, and pay special attention to winter in order to avoid the garden becoming dull and lifeless during that season. Wherever possible, try to choose plants which will provide interest in the garden for two or more seasons.

SPRING

At this exciting time of the year, the garden should be really sparkling, with new, fresh foliage in various colours appearing on deciduous trees and shrubs, and flowers opening on such plants as amelanchiers, camellias and rhododendrons (both of these require acid soil), magnolias, bergenias, primroses (*Primula*), pulmonarias, and bulbs. Ferns will be unfurling fresh green fronds in the dappled shade of either the woodland garden or the shrub border.

SPARKLING SPRING
Fresh foliage and bright flowers herald the arrival of spring. The shrubs here include deciduous azaleas, suitable only for acid soils.

Many trees will be looking very good, particularly the birches (*Betula*) with their haze of new green leaves. The young leaves of certain shrubs, notably *Photinia × fraseri* and pieris, are extremely colourful.

SUMMER

Most gardens are burgeoning with colour in the height of summer, when a wide range of hardy perennials really come into their own. There is plenty of scope for growing some of these in the low-maintenance garden – suitable plants include acanthus, hardy geraniums (cranesbills), and day lilies (*Hemerocallis*). Many shrubs will also be flowering at this time of year, including ceanothus, escallonias, and the shrubby cinquefoil (*Potentilla*); others, such as the

> ### Spring is a season of fresh growth and summer brings vibrant colour

smoke bush (*Cotinus* 'Grace'), will be decked in colourful foliage. Ornamental grasses interspersed with the shrubs and perennials serve to add welcome textural interest to the summer flower border.

AUTUMN

There is no shortage of colour for this interesting season. First there are the fiery foliage tints from trees and shrubs such as amelanchiers, acers – particularly Japanese maples (*Acer palmatum*) – and ornamental

WINTER FROSTING
The dead, bleached stems of ornamental grasses, the dead flowers of sedum, and the evergreen foliage of phormium are enhanced to perfection by a touch of frost, so make sure to include similar plants in your garden.

Prunus subhirtella 'Autumnalis', which will continue flowering right through the winter during prolonged spells of mild weather.

WINTER

At this time, evergreen shrubs really come into their own. Many have plain green leaves while others are brightly variegated, such as the spotted laurel (*Aucuba japonica* 'Crotonifolia'). Evergreen conifers also stand out in winter and come in all shades of green, plus blue and gold. Do not plant too many evergreens. A good balance in any mixed planting scheme is to have one-third evergreen shrubs and two-thirds deciduous shrubs. Many shrubs flower in winter; these include the witch hazels (*Hamamelis*), *Mahonia japonica*, and *Viburnum farreri*. The bark of a number of trees adds interest to the winter garden, particularly that of the snake-bark maple (*Acer davidii* 'Serpentine') and the paper-bark maple (*A. griseum*), as well as the birches, especially the Himalayan birch (*Betula utilis* var. *jacquemontii*).

cherries (*Prunus sargentii*). There are also berries and fruits from trees and shrubs; these include cotoneasters, crab apples (for example *Malus × zumi* 'Golden Hornet'), pyracanthas, and rowans (*Sorbus*). A number of trees come into flower during the autumn season, including the popular

ESSENTIAL SEASONAL TASKS

SPRING	SUMMER	AUTUMN	WINTER
• Carry out planting in early spring. • Top up any organic mulches. • If you have a lawn, you should start mowing. • Cut down dead stems and foliage of perennials. • Apply a general-purpose fertilizer around plants.	• Water your plants thoroughly during any prolonged periods of dry and drought conditions. • If you have a lawn, this is the season for regular mowing. You can employ someone to do this for you. • Trim formal hedges in late summer, using either shears or a hedge trimmer.	• Sweep up all the fallen leaves in the garden. You could compost these to produce leafmould, which makes a very good mulch. • Mow large lawns occasionally. • Pull up and discard the remains of any annual vegetables or flowering annuals.	• Ensure that any water features such as fountains are shut down for the winter. Remove and store pumps. • Carry out any pruning required on trees and shrubs.

LOW-MAINTENANCE GARDEN PLANS

PLANNING FOR A MINIMAL WORKLOAD

THE SIX PLANS THAT FOLLOW embrace a number of styles and themes to cater for most people's low-maintenance requirements. They can either be used in their entirety, if your garden is similar in size, or scaled down if it is smaller. The plans can also be adapted to suit your own garden or special area, and elements from different plans can be combined if you have the right conditions.

SUITING YOUR OWN NEEDS

Low-maintenance gardens come in many guises, as the plans on the following pages show. Gardens can either be formal, such as a paved one with a geometric design, or informal, like a woodland garden with more sweeping, flowing lines. The garden may have a cool atmosphere provided by a major water feature, or it may be warm and dry, as in the case of a gravel garden. The garden may be planned to suit the needs of a young family, a retired couple, or someone who can spare only one hour a week to maintain it. All the plans utilize a limited range of easy-care plants that often provide more than one season of interest.

TRANQUILLITY
A "living" area is an ever more important element in today's gardens, as people are making more of their plots for entertaining, alfresco meals, and general relaxation. Here, a combination of stone paving slabs and cobbles makes an attractive all-weather surface, and trellis screens covered in climbers provide the requisite privacy.

◀ SHAPE AND TEXTURE *These low-maintenance foliage plants make a pleasing combination.*

A Formal Paved Garden

Those people who say that a paved garden is not for real gardeners should take a look at this one. It is packed full of interesting plants – trees, shrubs, and perennials – including lots of bold, architectural specimens. The paving itself, consisting of natural stone slabs in varying sizes, relieved with brick, is very attractive, and it is further enhanced with plants. This particular plan is for a fairly large garden, but the idea can easily be adapted to fit a smaller area.

Mixed planting of shrubs and perennials for year-round interest, including architectural plants such as fatsias and phormiums

Timber pergola covering a living area, clothed with a maintenance-free climbing plant, such as the spring-flowering *Clematis montana*

Millstone bubble fountain with a surround of large, smooth pebbles, providing moving water yet safe for young children

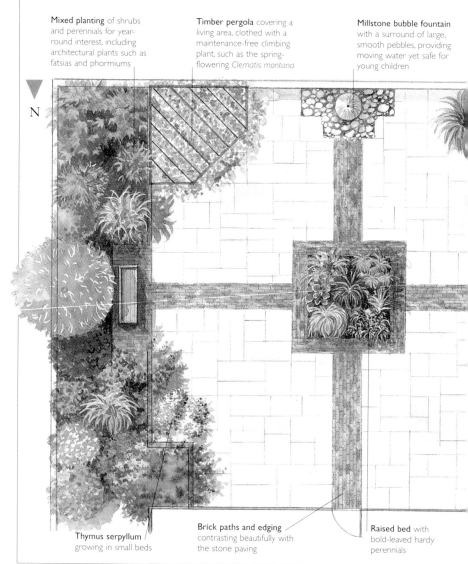

N

Thymus serpyllum growing in small beds

Brick paths and edging contrasting beautifully with the stone paving

Raised bed with bold-leaved hardy perennials

DESIGN BRIEF

- Formal design with attractive paving forming the open central area.
- Wide range of plants, including shrubs, perennials, and small trees, particularly bold, architectural ones.
- Raised bed to form a centrepiece on the paving.
- Pergola to cover an outdoor living area.

Ground-cover junipers spreading out onto the paving

Statue acting as a focal point

DESIGNING THE FLOOR

The plan shows expensive natural-stone paving, but there are other options for creating a hard "floor" (*see pp.14–15*). Your choice will depend on several aspects: what the garden will be used for, cost considerations, and the overall design style of the garden. In a formal garden, breaking up large, flat areas with varying colours, patterns, levels, and textures creates visual interest, and this can be done in a number of ways, using a range of complementary paving materials. Alternatively, for a bold, modern look, you could juxtapose brightly coloured paving setts with more traditional surfaces.

◀ VARYING PATTERNS
A mixture of shapes and textures can help to break up a large area visually. This is an effective combination of concrete paving slabs and pebbles set in concrete, edged with paving setts.

▼ CHANGING LEVELS
A timber decking floor is an attractive alternative to slabs and bricks. With decking, it is comparatively simple to create one or more changes of level, thereby adding interest to an otherwise flat garden.

A FORMAL GARDEN WITH WATER

THE CENTRAL GEOMETRIC WATER FEATURE forms a major aspect of this formal design. Many people think that adding water to a garden will result in a great deal of maintenance work, but this is not so if you avoid using aquatic plants, which need frequent attention. Although these do help to keep the water clear, proprietary algicides serve the same purpose. The water, and the surrounding plantings of lush foliage plants, create a cool, tranquil atmosphere.

Bamboos and grasses, *Phyllostachys nigra* (black bamboo) and *Miscanthus sinensis* cultivars, provide a lush, bold screen

Rill with mini-cascades – the plantings on either side are the ornamental grass blue fescue (*Festuca glauca*)

Concrete-block wall dividing the paved and gravel areas of the garden

A mini-cascade will provide the sound of moving water – there is another halfway along the rill, and a third at the far end

DESIGN BRIEF

• Pools at slightly different levels linked by a rill with mini-cascades. Water is circulated by a pump.
• Paving and gravel create the open areas.
• Lush plantings of grasses, bamboos, and ferns, plus a varied selection of other perennials and shrubs.
• Pierced concrete-block walls dividing the garden.
• Plenty of places to sit.

Lower pool, flush with the ground, edged with dwarf ornamental grasses and sedges (*Carex*), ferns, bergenias, hemerocallis, and astilbes

N

Seat placed on a paved area in a secluded corner

Gravel area for walking on

Paved area creating a maintenance-free open space, formed of pre-cast concrete paving slabs; in this area, seats provide places to relax

Mixed borders containing shrubs and perennials for all seasons, ornamental grasses, bamboos, and small trees including *Pyrus salicifolia* 'Pendula'

Upper raised pool, slightly higher in level than the pool at the far end; both have an edging of concrete paving slabs

Paved patio in front of the house

OTHER WATER FEATURES

Water features do not always have to be as ambitious as the one shown in the plan – you could opt for just one, maybe rectangular, shallow, unplanted pool, for example. They do not even have to be pools, however. Very fashionable in modern garden design are bubble fountains, which consist of water bubbling up through, say, a millstone or a bed of smooth pebbles. Water is circulated via an underground reservoir containing a pump. Wall-mounted spouts provide moving water in a similar way. Lion masks and gargoyles are popular, with a basin or small pool below.

RECTANGULAR POOL
Garden pools do not need to be deep to be effective. This is a comparatively safe pool if you have children in the family, because the water is extremely shallow, only just covering a bed of smooth pebbles. In the centre, water bubbles up constantly through the pebbles, being circulated via a reservoir and pump hidden below them. This type of low-maintenance pool would make a very pleasing feature on a formal patio.

LOG FOUNTAIN
Bubble fountains can take a number of forms. This very imaginative water feature has been created with sections of smooth timber poles.

OLD-FASHIONED PUMP
This reclaimed pump is now used as a spout, pouring a trickle of water into a raised pool. The planting is optional – it would look good without.

A Family Garden

THIS TYPE OF GARDEN generally has to cater for all ages, from toddlers to adults, so it needs play areas and spaces for outdoor living and relaxation. This design provides both. It is intentionally a simple, bold layout to allow for freedom of movement, and the garden is well planted with shrubs and ground-cover plants that have been carefully selected to give year-round interest and that will also withstand the rough and tumble of children playing.

Storage area, with a large shed for toys, bicycles, and garden tools, reached via a brick path through the shrubs

Birdbath in the centre of the paved area is of interest to all the family as it attracts wildlife

Mixed borders surrounding the paved area contain tough shrubs and ground-cover plants, including evergreens for year-round interest

Sandpit set in the patio very close to the house, so that adults can keep an eye on toddlers

N

DESIGN BRIEF

- Soft bark play area.
- Straight, hard path for bicycles and other wheels.
- Paved area for family living and ball games.
- Sandpit for toddlers (later turn into herb bed).
- Storage area for bicycles, toys, and other items.
- Dense plantings of child-proof plants.

Play area surfaced with soft play bark

Ornamental grasses are included, such as *Miscanthus sinensis* 'Variegatus'

Tough plants in the surrounding borders include various bamboos such as the non-spreading umbrella bamboo (*Fargesia murieliae*)

Random-stone paving creating an open area in the garden which is used for family living and children's games

Straight brick path used to access the play area and for riding bicycles

Patio constructed of concrete paving slabs

CHOOSING PLANTS AND SURFACES

In the plan, ground-cover plants that do not mind being trodden on have been used alongside the path and at the front of borders. These include *Hypericum calycinum*, *Juniperus horizontalis* 'Wiltonii', *Stachys byzantina* 'Big Ears', *Pachysandra terminalis*, *Salix purpurea* 'Nana', *Lonicera pileata*, *Vinca minor* cultivars, *Hedera helix* 'Glacier', and *Euonymus fortunei* 'Emerald 'n' Gold'. For growing in the middle and back of the borders choose tough shrubs such as those shown in the picture below. The two small trees selected to provide shade are *Malus floribunda* (*top left*) and *Acer negundo* 'Flamingo' (*top right*).

◀ STRONG SHRUBS
Ceanothus 'Puget Blue' (left), Choisya 'Aztec Pearl' (centre), and Lonicera nitida 'Baggesen's Gold' (right) are all resilient.

▼ SOFT MATERIALS
A deep layer of soft play bark makes a suitable surface for children's play areas.

AN INFORMAL GRAVEL GARDEN

WITH THIS DESIGN THE ENTIRE GARDEN is gravelled, including the beds and borders, which have a geotextile sheet (*see p.63*) underneath the gravel to suppress weeds and help retain moisture. A gravel garden is not the best choice for a family, because young children may be inclined to throw handfuls of gravel around. It is to be recommended, though, for a dry, sunny garden, planted with a good quantity of drought-tolerant plants.

Timber pergola climber, covering living area

N

Mixed planting that includes the small golden tree honey locust (*Gleditsia tria-canthos* 'Sunburst'), the grass *Helicto-trichon semper-virens*, and various shrubby potentillas

Stepping stones, formed of concrete paving slabs sunk into the ground, create an attractive path through the gravelled area

Mixed shrub planting that includes *Genista lydia, Ceanothus thyrsiflorus, Hibiscus syriacus, Lavandula angustifolia* 'Hidcote', phormiums, and *Yucca flaccida* 'Ivory'

Coarse-grade stone or natural-stone chippings creating a variation in texture throughout the gravelled area

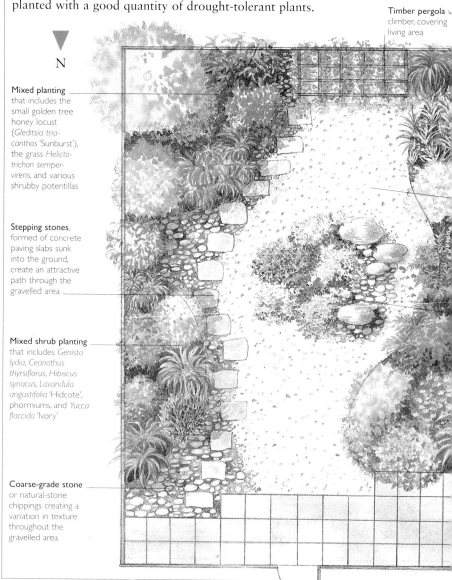

DESIGN BRIEF

- Whole garden gravelled, including beds and borders.
- Variation in surfacing.
- Open area in the centre, with stepping stones.
- Paved patio next to house.
- Pergola over living area.
- Bold plantings, including grasses and spiky plants.
- Extensive range of drought-tolerant plants.

Cockspur thorn (*Crataegus crus-galli*), a small tree

Colutea arborescens is a drought-tolerant shrub

Gravelled area, used for walking through the garden, made of pea shingle (smooth, water-worn, dredged shingle). It can also be used as a mulch on the borders

Collection of low-growing thymes (*Thymus serpyllum*) with aromatic foliage, edged with coarse-grade stone and outcrops of rock

Mixed planting that includes ground-cover junipers, the small tree *Robinia pseudoacacia* 'Frisia', the shrub *Elaeagnus* x *ebbingei*, and the perennials *Acanthus spinosus*, *Achillea* 'Moonshine', and *Sisyrinchium striatum*

Paved patio in front of the house

DESIGNING WITH GRAVEL

Instead of having a large expanse of one type of gravel, which can be monotonous, in order to create a variation in texture you can add areas of other materials such as smooth pebbles, coarse-grade stone (natural-stone chippings), and even outcrops of flat specimen rocks. These, of course, are for decorative effect only and are not intended for walking on. Glass "gravel" is an innovation that provides bright colour.

▲ GLASS GRAVEL
This new material for modern gardens is available in various colours, and is used for paths and small decorative areas.

◀ PEBBLES
These can be used in drifts to add textural variety to a gravelled area. They look good with grassy plants.

▼ SHINGLE
Pea shingle covering a walking area can be nicely broken up with areas of spiky plants and smooth pebbles.

A Woodland Garden

CREATING A WOODLAND GARDEN is an excellent idea if you have moisture-retentive soil, especially if there are existing trees to provide the necessary dappled shade. If not, small trees such as birches, maples, flowering cherries, and rowans can be planted in groups. There is a wealth of fine woodland plants to choose from. Overall, this is a cool, shady garden which would fit well into a rural or well-wooded area, and if heavily mulched is very low in maintenance.

Groups of small ornamental trees provide dappled shade for the woodland plants

The fernery, shaded by a Japanese maple (*Acer palmatum*), contains a number of hardy ferns such as *Athyrium, Dryopteris,* and *Polystichum*

Ground-cover planting with drifts of dwarf grasses and similar plants such as *Festuca, Molinia,* and sedge (*Carex*)

DESIGN BRIEF

• Groups of small, airy trees such as birches and maples to create dappled shade.
• Underplantings of shade-loving woodland shrubs, perennials, and bulbs.
• Meandering paths through the woodland area.
• Fernery with a varied collection of hardy ferns.
• Central open area of gravel and low-growing ground-cover plants.
• Split-level timber decking terrace adjacent to house.

Small ornamental trees including the snake-bark maple (*Acer davidii*) and its cultivars, with unusual green and white striated bark and good autumn leaf colour

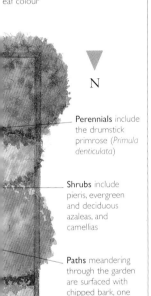

N

Perennials include the drumstick primrose (*Primula denticulata*)

Shrubs include pieris, evergreen and deciduous azaleas, and camellias

Paths meandering through the garden are surfaced with chipped bark, one of the most natural-looking materials

Gravelled area to create the essential open space in the centre of the garden, softened at the edges with a variety of ground-cover plants

Ground-cover planting with low-growing junipers such as *Juniperus horizontalis* and *J. sabina* 'Tamariscifolia', plus dwarf bamboo *Sasa veitchii*

Split-level decking next to the house

PLANTING FOR NATURAL EFFECT

A woodland garden has various levels of plants, starting with trees, the tallest, then shrubs, then shorter perennials, and finally prostrate ground-cover plants and dwarf spring bulbs at the lowest level. The shrubs are grown as single specimen plants, or on a larger scale in groups of three or more, and the perennials, bulbs, and other shorter plants are then planted in informal drifts around and between them.

◄ GROUND COVER
Use carpeting plants such as these bugle (Ajuga) *cultivars for a tapestry effect.*

▼ FERNERY
These ferns create a delightfully lush, cool effect in the shade of a woodland garden.

AN HOUR-A-WEEK GARDEN

THIS GARDEN IS FOR PEOPLE who have minimal time to spare for maintenance but who still want a garden that is colourful in summer when it is likely to be used the most. It incorporates a secluded natural area that is ideal for sitting and relaxing in, while the hard surfacing is suitable for entertaining and alfresco meals. The main regular task in spring and summer is mowing the grass paths. The long grass needs to be cut only once a year, during the summer.

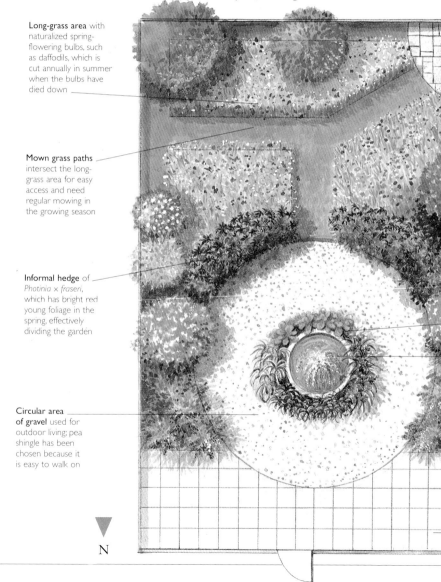

Long-grass area with naturalized spring-flowering bulbs, such as daffodils, which is cut annually in summer when the bulbs have died down

Mown grass paths intersect the long-grass area for easy access and need regular mowing in the growing season

Informal hedge of *Photinia × fraseri*, which has bright red young foliage in the spring, effectively dividing the garden

Circular area of gravel used for outdoor living; pea shingle has been chosen because it is easy to walk on

N

DESIGN BRIEF

- A patio situated right in front of the house.
- A gravel area creating an open centre for the garden.
- An easy-care water feature.
- Borders of easy-care shrubs and perennials that provide plenty of colour in summer when the garden is being frequently used.
- Small ornamental trees that provide dappled shade.
- A natural-looking area.
- A secluded place in which to sit and relax at any time.

Covered seat on a paved area

Small trees include the cockspur thorn (*Crataegus crus-galli*), which has spring flowers, red fruit, and autumn colour

Plants around the pool are *Carex oshimensis* 'Evergold', *Bergenia* 'Silberlicht', yellow day lilies (*Hemerocallis*), and black-leaved *Ophiopogon planiscapus* 'Nigrescens', all creating a lush effect

Raised pool with a central fountain creating a pleasing focal point; the pool is not planted with labour-intensive aquatic plants

Mixed borders containing shrubs, hardy perennials, and low-growing ground-cover plants including prostrate junipers

Paved patio adjacent to the house

EASY-CARE PLANTS

The mixed borders contain a range of spring- and summer-flowering shrubs that do not need regular pruning; these include shrubby veronicas (*Hebe*), Juneberry (*Amelanchier lamarckii*), viburnums, and escallonias. Small trees include the spring-flowering Japanese crab apple (*Malus floribunda*) and Hubei rowan (*Sorbus hupehensis*) with white, flushed pink, berries in autumn. Self-supporting hardy perennials are mixed in. The bulbs in the long-grass area need no attention.

SPRING BLOOMS
Bergenias are evergreen spring-flowering perennials that produce white, pink, or rose-red flowers and have bold, shiny, leathery leaves.

SPRING FOLIAGE
Photinia × fraseri *is an evergreen shrub whose young spring leaves are bronze or bright red. There are several cultivars to choose from.*

AUTUMN BERRIES
The guelder rose (Viburnum opulus) has white summer blooms followed by red autumn berries and foliage. 'Compactum' grows slowly.

YEAR-ROUND FOLIAGE
Sasa veitchii *is a pleasing dwarf bamboo that spreads only moderately. The leaf edges wither and then turn straw-coloured in winter.*

GETTING DOWN TO BASICS

MAKING THE MOST OF YOUR SOIL

YOU MAY NEED TO PUT IN quite a lot of work at the beginning in order to create your ideal low-maintenance garden, but you will certainly reap the rewards later. One of the most important tasks initially is to improve your soil before planting. When the garden is completed, there will inevitably be a few minor maintenance tasks such as watering, mulching, feeding, and pruning.

IMPROVING THE SOIL

To reduce future weed problems, perennial weeds (*see p.63*) must be eradicated first. The most efficient method is spraying with a systemic weedkiller such as glyphosate. This must be applied when the weeds are in full growth – follow the manufacturer's instructions to the letter. Alternatively, remove the weeds, including roots, during digging, but this is less efficient and any roots left behind will produce more weeds.

When you are satisfied that the weeds are dead, the soil for all planting areas should be dug. During digging, add bulky organic matter, such as garden compost, well-rotted manure, or composted shredded bark. This will help well-drained soils, such as sand and chalk, to retain moisture, and will open up and improve the drainage of heavy clay soils. If you have the latter type, also add copious amounts of horticultural grit or coarse sand to improve drainage further.

1 When digging, open up a trench that is 30cm (12in) wide and the depth of a spade blade (called a "spit"). Add a 5–7cm (2–3in) layer of well-rotted organic matter.

2 Thoroughly fork this organic matter into the bottom of the trench. The action will also help to break up the soil, which may well have become compacted.

3 Dig another trench behind the first one, using the soil to refill it. Repeat the process until the whole area has been dug. Let the soil settle for a few months before planting.

◄ FLOURISHING PLANTS *This informal planting scheme makes good use of alchemilla and grasses.*

DRAWING UP PLANS

WHEN CREATING A GARDEN it is important to carry out an initial survey of the existing site and to draw up a new plan before you begin any construction work or planting. It is worth taking accurate measurements and drawing a plan to scale if you are to end up with a design that works for you from the start and will not need any alterations later. The following techniques will help to ensure that your new plan can be easily transferred to your plot.

SURVEYING YOUR PLOT

Before starting to design your new garden, it is advisable to make a simple survey of any existing garden features you may have, including details of the side of the house that faces the garden. This survey will help you later when you are drawing up a new plan. You are going to need a couple of measuring tapes – ideally one of 30m (100ft) for long measurements and one of 3m (10ft) for short ones – plus some sheets of paper, a clipboard, and a pencil for sketching out your rough survey.

First, draw in the boundaries of the garden, then make a freehand sketch of everything in it, as shown in the example below. For convenience, start with the house, marking the positions of the windows and doors. Then include any outbuildings such as the garden shed or garage. Finally, add in all the garden features – trees, hedges, flower beds, shrub borders, water features, and so forth, and give them brief labels. Now add the datum lines and take all the relevant measurements, adding them to the survey.

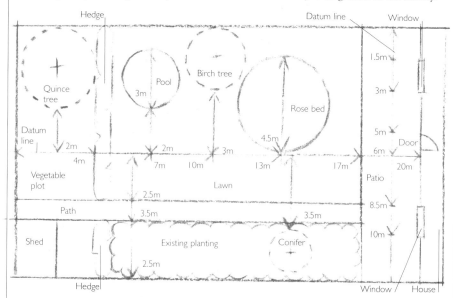

MAKING A SURVEY SKETCH
Two "datum lines" will be required from which to take sets of measurements. One of these runs the length of the garden (through the middle), and the other runs across the width and near to the house, so that the door and window sizes can easily be marked. Draw the datum lines on the sketch and label them.

DECIDING WHAT TO KEEP

In order to convert an established garden into a low-maintenance one, it may be necessary to remove or replace many of the existing features; but it is worth being quite ruthless at the planning stage if eventually you are to have a garden that fits the bill.

Keep as many of the larger plants as you possibly can, so that your garden retains a mature appearance. It is well worth keeping any existing trees, since these are all low in maintenance. Consider the shrubs in some detail, however, because many of these are likely to need regular pruning; retain only those that do not demand such attention. You may decide to convert the lawn into an area of gravel or paving, since grass usually requires a great deal of work to keep it looking at its best. A boundary hedge that only needs clipping once a year is worth retaining, but high-maintenance hedges should always be replaced. Remove such features as rock gardens, herbaceous borders, and annual bedding schemes, which are all very labour-intensive.

▲ DEMANDING ROSES
Rose types such as climbers, hybrid teas, and floribundas all need complex annual pruning, deadheading, and spraying.

▶ ATTRACTIVE TO SLUGS
Hostas are not a practical proposition for the low-maintenance garden because much effort is required to keep slugs and snails at bay.

PLANTS TO AVOID

Hedging plants (such as privet) that need clipping more than once in the growing season.
Annual bedding plants – planting these out is time-consuming, and has to be carried out twice a year. They also need dead-heading.
Annuals – these have to be grown from seeds every year, and the subsequent seedlings and plants require a lot of care.
Herbaceous plants (hardy perennials) that are likely to need staking and tying to prevent them flopping over in the border.
Rock plants or alpines on a rock garden – weeding between them is time-consuming.

TRIANGULATION

In order to pinpoint the exact position of a tree easily when making a survey sketch, take a couple of measurements from two fixed points, such as the corners of the house, to the trunk of the relevant tree, and add these to the sketch, using a pair of compasses. The point at which the two lines cross will give you the precise position of the tree. This is known as the triangulation method.

MAKING A NEW PLAN

On completion of the survey, when all garden features have been measured and included in the survey sketch (*see p.58*), you need to make important decisions regarding what to retain and what to get rid of. As you can see from glancing at the rough plan below, very little has been retained from the original survey sketch, because many features of the original garden required a lot of maintenance. All of these have been removed to make way for your chosen easy-care options.

Other information you can include on the rough plan that may affect your design is the passage of the sun, any shadows that may be cast by surrounding buildings, the direction of prevailing winds, good and bad views, and the direction of any slopes. The retained features should be transferred onto a final scale drawing (known as the base plan); by far the easiest method is to plot them onto graph paper. Once the base plan has reached this stage, you can add in all the new low-maintenance features.

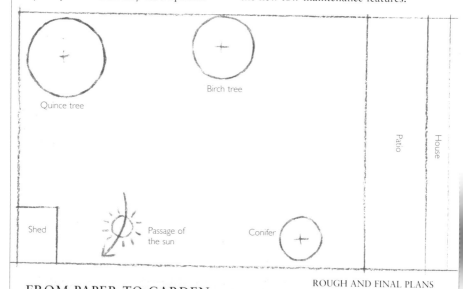

Quince tree

Birch tree

Patio

House

Shed

Passage of the sun

Conifer

FROM PAPER TO GARDEN

• The last stage of all is transferring the final detailed scale plan to the garden itself.

• Run a line down the centre of the garden, at right angles to the house, corresponding to the datum line shown in the survey sketch (*see p.58*) and make all your measurements from this. In a split-level garden, a line can be laid on each level.

• The outline of the plan can be marked on the ground using dry sand in a plastic drinks bottle poured out in narrow lines.

• Adopt a logical sequence when marking out. For example, start from the house and work towards the end of the garden.

• If the garden has several levels, it is best to mark out one level completely before going on to the next.

• A work schedule is useful if the work is to be undertaken over a period of time, preferably starting nearest to the house.

ROUGH AND FINAL PLANS
The survey sketch (see p.58) *and rough plan showing the garden features to be retained* (see above) *are used to draw the final plan to scale. It is a good idea to overlay the final plan with tracing paper and draw the new features onto this, to enable you to make changes easily without spoiling the final plan. When you are satisfied, transfer the features to the master plan.*

VISUALIZING THE RESULTS

Many professional garden designers prepare a perspective drawing to give their clients a fair idea of how their garden will look when it is finished. The drawing of a low-maintenance garden below gives you an idea of how to go about it, but it does not have to be as professional as this. You do not have to be an accomplished artist, and it can be fun to draw up; it will certainly help you to imagine how the garden will look, particularly from the house, when it is completed. Instead of drawing in lots of detail, you could just draw simple outlines for each major feature and plant.

PRACTICAL TIPS

• A perspective drawing can be prepared using water-colour paints, coloured pencils, or crayons.

• Keep it simple. There is certainly no need to put a lot of detail into the plants, as in this drawing.

• First, lightly sketch out all the shapes with a pencil – the basic shapes (*see right*) are more important than fine detail.

• The plants should be drawn to their mature sizes, even if they are very slow-growing, so take care to check what these are.

• Finally, fill in the shapes with appropriate colours. For plants grown primarily for their flowers, use flower rather than foliage colour.

Garden shed doubles up as a summer house and focal point

Utility-grade lawn with paved mowing edge, simple to mow and maintain

Paved area extends halfway down the garden

Borders with easy-care shrubs, and ground-cover plants at the front

Patio containers planted with permanent plants so that they should need relatively little care

Maintenance Techniques

ALTHOUGH LOW-MAINTENANCE GARDENS need minimal attention, several aspects of plant care still need to be considered. These include: watering when required to ensure that young plants establish quickly and to keep older plants growing during dry periods; mulching to prevent the growth of weeds; feeding to ensure optimum growth and flowering; occasional pruning of shrubs and trees; and routine trimming of certain hedges and ground-cover plants.

WATERING

The easiest way to water plants growing in borders is to set up a permanent watering system connected to a tap. Popular and economical is the seep hose (*see right*), which is laid on the ground between the plants. For containers, it is best to use a permanent drip system, consisting of thin pipes sprouting from a main pipe. Fit a timer to the tap for economical watering.

The hose is micro-porous

Connection for supply hose

End stop

WHEN YOU ARE AWAY

• A low-maintenance garden should look after itself, but it is still advisable to ask a neighbour to keep an eye on things, especially plants that might need watering in dry spells.
• If you have a lawn, mow it just before you depart. It should be fine for 10–14 days.

SEEP HOSE
Water gradually oozes out of the seep hose and gently soaks into the surrounding soil.

1 **Lay the seep hose** in loops around your plants, allowing for it to moisten a 38cm (15in) band of soil. Since it does not readily lie flat, peg it down wherever required with hoops made from thick galvanized wire.

2 **Hide the hose** by covering it with a 5cm (2in) layer of mulch, such as chipped bark or gravel. This not only creates an attractive finish but also suppresses weeds and prevents rapid drying out of the soil in the border.

MULCHING TO SUPPRESS WEEDS

Using mulches inhibits the growth of weeds by starving them of light, keeps soil moist, and creates an attractive finish. Organic mulches are chipped bark, garden compost, and well-rotted manure; mineral mulches include gravel and pebbles; sheet mulches are usually black polythene which, unless perforated, does not let air and water pass through, or permeable "geotextiles", such as bonded fibre fleece or woven polypropylene, which does. Sheet mulches are often covered with an organic or mineral mulch. Geotextile mulches can be used beneath paving and gravel to suppress weeds.

1 **When planting** through geotextile sheet mulch, lay the sheets (overlap if need be) over prepared soil that has been raked smooth and level.

2 **Place the plants** on the sheet mulch at the correct spacings. These are *Euonymus fortunei* 'Emerald 'n' Gold', spaced 30cm (12in) apart.

3 **To plant,** make two cuts, 15–20cm (6–8in) long, and at right angles, through the sheet. Fold the flaps beneath the sheet to expose the soil.

4 **Make a hole** for planting. The top of the rootball should be at soil level. Fill in with soil around the plant and firm it well.

5 **After planting,** pull out the four flaps in the sheet around each plant and replace them so that they come right up to the plant stems.

6 **Finally, add** a 5cm (2in) layer of organic or mineral mulch to hide as well as hold down the sheet mulch. Here pea shingle is being used.

PERENNIAL WEEDS

The following are some of the most rampant weeds – most of them have either vigorous, creeping or deep roots, and they must be eradicated before preparing beds for planting (*see p.57*). Remember that they are extremely persistent, and therefore it may require more than one application of weedkiller in order to remove them completely.

Couch grass (*Elymus repens*)
Creeping thistle (*Cirsium arvense*)
Creeping yellow cress (*Rorippa sylvestris*)
Field bindweed (*Convolvulus arvensis*)
Ground elder (*Aegopodium podagraria*)
Horsetail (*Equisetum arvense*)
Perennial stinging nettle (*Urtica dioica*)

FEEDING YOUR PLANTS

All garden plants, including trees, shrubs, perennials, and even bulbs, benefit from being given regular applications of fertilizer to promote optimum growth and flowering. This could become a time-consuming task, so it is best to apply fertilizer only once a year, using a slow-release type. It should be applied in spring just before or just as growth is starting. Spring-flowering bulbs should be fed immediately after flowering by applying a general-purpose liquid fertilizer. This helps to build up their reserves, which in turn ensures that they will flower well in the following year.

1 **When applying** fertilizer around plants, first scrape back any mulching material, then scatter the granules as evenly as possible.

2 **Afterwards, replace** the mulching material, and in the case of organic mulches, such as this chipped bark, top up if necessary.

PLANT FOOD

• The usual method of feeding garden plants today is to use a general-purpose, slow-release fertilizer, which releases its plant foods gradually and steadily over the whole growing season.
• Slow-release fertilizers usually come in granular form, but some may be in the form of powder, such as the organic food known as blood, fish, and bone.
• Slow-release fertilizers are also available in the form of tablets or spikes, which are inserted in holes around the plant. These are ideal for feeding plants growing in containers, raised beds, and other small areas.

TRIMMING HEDGES AND GROUND COVER

Most hedge trimming is carried out once a year in late summer as growth is slowing down. For small-leaved hedging plants such as beech (*Fagus sylvatica*) or hornbeam (*Carpinus betulus*), use shears or a powered hedge-trimmer. For large-leaved plants, such as cherry laurel (*Prunus laurocerasus*), cut individual shoots with secateurs. Some ground-cover plants, such as epimediums and rose of Sharon (*Hypericum calycinum*), should be sheared to the ground in spring.

CUT HARD BACK AFTER FLOWERING
This epimedium is being cut to the ground immediately after flowering. It will be stimulated to produce a crop of new shoots.

PRUNING ESTABLISHED SHRUBS AND TREES

The trees and shrubs recommended in this book, as well as other low-maintenance kinds, do not require regular pruning. Occasional pruning may be necessary, however, especially for older specimens. Look out for for dead and dying wood, and remove it completely as soon as you notice it, irrespective of the time of year. If left, it could spread disease, which may then affect the rest of the plant. As far as trees are concerned, that is all you need to do; but shrubs may need more attention. As they become older, some of the oldest wood can either be cut out completely or pruned back to encourage the production of new shoots. The oldest wood will be found in the centre of the plant, and removing some of this will open up the shrub and let in light and air, which in turn will encourage better growth. This type of pruning can be carried out in winter, ideally in late winter just before the plants start into new growth. Some shrubs benefit from being cut back occasionally if they start to become "leggy"; one good example of this is mahonia, shown below. This pruning is best done after flowering, and the plants will then produce new shoots from the cut-back stems.

1 To prune a leggy shrub like this winter-flowering mahonia, use sharp secateurs. Cut back old stems just after they have flowered.

2 The pruned stems will start to produce vigorous new shoots in the spring, and these should then flower in the following year.

3 The same shrub also has some old stems, declining in vigour, in the centre. Using a pruning saw, cut back some of these very hard.

4 Removing old wood in stages over several years lets light and air right into the centre of the shrub; here the first stem has been removed.

PRUNING TIPS

• When you are pruning shrubs and trees, always use very sharp tools to ensure really clean, smooth cuts which will heal up much more quickly than the ragged cuts that are produced by blunt implements.

• A pair of good-quality parrot-bill secateurs is recommended for light pruning tasks. These are better than the anvil type, which are inclined to crush plant stems.

• A pruning saw, either one with a curved blade or the type with a blade that folds into the handle, will be needed for cutting old, thick wood.

• Garden shears can be used for trimming both hedges and ground-cover plants. Again, the blades should be extremely sharp. Alternatively, you can use a powered hedge-trimmer if it is necessary to speed up the job.

LABOUR-SAVING PLANT CHOICES

THESE PLANTS ARE TROUBLE-FREE and need minimum maintenance. Most do not need regular pruning; others, such as some perennials, require annual cutting down. All the perennials are hardy and self-supporting. The symbols given at the end of each entry indicate the plant's preferred growing conditions.

☒ *Prefers full sun* ☒ *Prefers partial shade* ☀ *Tolerates full shade* ◊ *Prefers well-drained soil* ◊ *Prefers moist soil* ❋❋❋ *Fully hardy (down to –15°C/5°F)* ❋❋ *Frost-hardy (down to –5°C/23°F)* ♀ *RHS Award of Garden Merit*

TREES

SMALL ORNAMENTAL TREES should be included in every garden, except the tiniest sites, because they help to form a permanent framework. They also provide dappled shade, which is loved by many of the smaller plants, and are useful for screening any unsightly objects beyond the garden boundary. The dense evergreen foliage of conifers contrasts well with deciduous trees.

Acer (Maple)
Acers or maples are mainly deciduous trees of diverse habit, grown for attractive foliage or bark. *A. davidii* 'Serpentine' ♀, a snake-bark maple, has green and white striped bark. In autumn the leaves turn orange to yellow. This maple is especially recommended for woodland gardens. Height and spread 15m (50ft). *A. griseum* ♀ (Paper-bark maple), with its peeling orange-brown bark, makes a fine specimen tree. The leaves take on fiery tints in autumn. It is rather slow-growing, but eventually

ACER PALMATUM

attains a height and spread of 10m (30ft). The leaves of *A. negundo* 'Flamingo' ♀

(Box elder) have pink edges that turn white in summer. This is a very good specimen tree, especially for modern and town or city gardens. Height 15m (50ft), spread 10m (30ft). *A. palmatum* (Japanese maple) and its many cultivars are excellent for autumn leaf colour. It needs shelter from cold winds, which can scorch the foliage, and therefore is a good subject for woodland gardens. Height and spread are variable. Maples will grow in any moist soil in sun or partial shade.
☒ – ☒ ◊ ❋❋❋

◀ A GRAVEL GARDEN *At the height of summer, this gravel garden presents a stunning display.*

Betula utilis var. **jacque-montii** ♀ (Himalayan birch)
This is a deciduous tree with glistening white bark. One of the finest birches for small gardens, it can be grown as a single specimen or planted in groups to create a woodland garden. It is suitable for exposed situations and any type of soil in full sun or partial shade. Height 18m (60ft), spread 10m (30ft).
◨ – ◙ ◊ ✿ ✿ ✿

Malus (Crab apple)
Crab apples are deciduous trees that are grown for their flowers or decorative fruits. *M. floribunda* ♀ has light pink flowers arising from red buds in mid- to late spring. Height and spread 10m (30ft). One of the best for fruits is *M. × zumi* 'Golden Hornet' ♀. White spring flowers are followed by long-lasting deep yellow fruits. Height 10m (30ft), spread 8m (25ft). Both are excellent specimen trees for any garden soil.
◨ ◊ ✿ ✿ ✿
Also recommended:
M. tschonoskii ♀

MALUS FLORIBUNDA

PRUNUS SARGENTII

Prunus (Ornamental cherry)
Ornamental cherries are deciduous trees grown for flowers, autumn leaf colour, or attractive bark. *P. serrula* ♀ has peeling red-brown bark and white flowers in spring. Height and spread 10m (50ft). *P. × subhirtella* 'Autumnalis' ♀ is grown for its white flowers that are produced between autumn and spring; height and spread 8m (25ft). *P. × s.* 'Autumnalis Rosea' ♀ has pink flowers. The leaves of *P. sargentii* ♀ take on fiery tints in autumn. Height 20m (70ft), spread 15m (50ft).
◨ ◊ ✿ ✿ ✿

Pyrus salicifolia 'Pendula' ♀ (Weeping silver pear)
This deciduous weeping tree has beautiful, willow-like, silver-grey leaves. It makes a superb specimen tree and is ideal for creating a focal point in a garden, so try growing it in isolation. This is one of the best ornamental trees for a small garden, and is at home in both town and country. It will grow in any well-drained garden soil. Height 5m (15ft), spread 4m (12ft).
◨ ◊ ✿ ✿ ✿

Robinia pseudoacacia 'Frisia' ♀ (False acacia)
A deciduous columnar tree with golden yellow leaves that become green in summer and orange-yellow in autumn. It is fast-growing and a fine specimen tree, especially for urban gardens. It looks good in modern settings and gravel gardens. This tree is drought-tolerant, and needs shelter from strong winds. Height 15m (50ft), spread 8m (25ft).
◨ ◊ ✿ ✿ ✿

Sorbus (Rowan, mountain ash)
These deciduous trees are grown mainly for their fine autumn fruits. *S. hupehensis* ♀ has white berries flushed with pink. In autumn the leaves turn red. Height and spread 8m (25ft). *S. aucuparia* 'Beissneri' has copper bark, orange-red berries, and yellow leaf tints in autumn. Height 10m (30ft), spread 5m (15ft). *S. americana* has orange-red berries. Good for both woodland and town gardens, these rowans grow in any soil, ideally acid to neutral.
◨ – ◙ ◊ ✿ ✿ ✿

PYRUS SALICIFOLIA 'PENDULA'

CONIFERS

Chamaecyparis lawson-iana (Lawson cypress)
This is a narrowly columnar or conical evergreen tree, which is relatively fast-growing. Good cultivars include 'Ellwoodii' ♚, with blue-grey leaves, height 3m (10ft); 'Pembury Blue' ♚, with bright blue-grey leaves, height 15m (50ft); and flame-shaped 'Erecta Aurea' with golden foliage, height 12–15m (40–50ft). All make fine specimen trees. Any moist soil is suitable, and preferably acid to neutral.
◙ ◊ ✿ ✿ ✿

Chamaecyparis pisifera (Sawara cypress)
A broad, conical, evergreen tree. 'Boulevard' ♚ has blue-green leaves, height 10m (30ft), and 'Filifera Aurea' ♚ has golden-yellow leaves and pendulous thread-like shoots, height 12m (40ft). They make good specimen trees. Any moist soil is suitable, preferably acid to neutral.
◙ ◊ ✿ ✿ ✿

CHAMAECYPARIS LAWSONIANA
'PEMBURY BLUE'

Cupressus macrocarpa (Monterey cypress)
A large, evergreen, narrowly conical or columnar conifer, making a fine specimen or hedge plant. Height to 30m (100ft), spread 4m (12ft). Golden-yellow 'Goldcrest' ♚ is much smaller. Shelter from cold, drying winds.
◙ ◊ ✿ ✿ ✿

Juniperus (Juniper)
Many low-growing junipers make excellent ground cover, including *J. horizontalis* 'Wiltonii' ♚, with glaucous foliage, height 30cm (12in), indefinite spread; *J. sabina* 'Tamariscifolia', with bright green leaves, height 1–2m (3–6ft), spread 1.5–2m (5–6ft); and *J. squamata* 'Blue Star' ♚, with silver-blue leaves, height 40cm (16in), spread 1m (3ft). All junipers are drought-tolerant.
◙ – ◙ ◊ ✿ ✿ ✿
J. × *pfitzeriana* 'Gold Coast', see p.13. Also recommended: *J. rigida* subsp. *conferta* (Shore juniper)

Pinus mugo (Dwarf mountain pine)
Many pines are too large for most gardens, but this one is ideal for smaller sites. It forms a neat, rounded shape and has dense, deep or bright green needles. Height 3.5m (11ft), spread 5m (15ft). It makes a superb specimen plant, and is well suited to gravel gardens. Grow it in any well-drained soil.
◙ ◊ ✿ ✿ ✿

Thuja occidentalis 'Rheingold' ♚
This is a cone-shaped form of the white cedar, growing up to 2m (6ft) in height and spread, with gold evergreen foliage. The leaves are pink-tinted when young. It is a very effective conifer when used as a specimen plant in a formal setting, and is an essential ingredient in a bed of small conifers. It prefers a moist soil in full sun, and needs to be sheltered from cold, drying winds.
◙ ◊ ✿ ✿ ✿

JUNIPERUS SQUAMATA
'BLUE STAR'

THUJA OCCIDENTALIS
'RHEINGOLD'

SHRUBS AND CLIMBING PLANTS

YOU CAN USE SHRUBS TO PROVIDE a strong framework for the garden and, if carefully selected, they will ensure both colour and interest over all four seasons. Climbers are ideal for providing interest on a higher level, whether it is a wall, fence, or pergola. Many shrubs and climbers, especially the deciduous flowering kinds, need regular annual pruning, but all those recommended here, except *Hypericum* and *Ruscus*, do not require this time-consuming task.

AMELANCHIER LAMARCKII

Amelanchier lamarckii ♀
(Juneberry)
The leaves of *A. lamarckii*, a dual-season deciduous shrub, open bronze, turn dark green, then take on fiery tints in autumn. Masses of white flowers in mid-spring are followed by edible, purple-black berries. Height 10m (30ft), spread 14m (46ft). Ideal for a shrub border or a woodland garden. Grow in moisture-retentive, acid soil.
☼ – ◙ ◊ ❋ ❋ ❋

Aucuba japonica 'Crotoni-folia' ♀ (Spotted laurel)
An evergreen shrub whose large leaves are speckled with yellow. This female cultivar bears red berries in autumn if there is a male plant, such as 'Golden King', nearby. Height

and spread 3m (10ft). This shrub makes a handsome informal hedge, for town, city, or coastal gardens.
▣ ◊ ❋ ❋ ❋

Camellia × williamsii
There are numerous forms of *C. × williamsii*; 'Donation' ♀ with its freely produced, semi-double, pink flowers from late winter to late spring is an outstanding one. A compact evergreen shrub, height 5m (15ft), spread 2.5m (8ft), it makes an impact in the shrub border or woodland garden. Grow it in acid, moisture-retentive, humus-rich soil ideally in partial shade.
◙ ◊ ❋ ❋ ❋
Also recommended:
C. japonica cultivars

AUCUBA JAPONICA 'CROTONIFOLIA'

COTINUS 'GRACE'

Ceanothus thyrsiflorus
(Blueblossom)
This evergreen shrub produces light to deep blue flowers in spring. It is fast-growing, with a height and spread of 6m (20ft). *C. t.* var. *repens* ♀ is only 1m (3ft) high with a 2.5m (8ft) spread, and makes good ground cover. Any well-drained soil, including chalk, is suitable. Provide shelter from cold, drying winds.
▣ ◊ ❋ ❋ ❋
C. 'Puget Blue' ♀, *see p.49*

Cotinus 'Grace' ♀
(Smoke bush)
A deciduous shrub with rounded, purple leaves which become brilliant red in autumn. Height 6m (20ft), spread 5m (15ft). Grow this dual-season plant in a shrub

Ruscus aculeatus
(Butcher's broom)
This clump-forming evergreen shrub will grow in partial or even deep shade with dry soil, and makes excellent ground cover. It has flat, leaf-like, spiny, deep green shoots, and bears red berries in autumn and winter if male and female, or hermaphrodite, plants are grown. Height 75cm (30in), spread 1m (3ft). Cut out dead stems in spring. Grow in any well-drained soil.
◫ – ☀ ◊ ❋ ❋ ❋

SKIMMIA JAPONICA 'RUBELLA'

Skimmia japonica
This evergreen shrub, of rounded habit, is grown for its white flowers and red berries. Male and female flowers are borne on separate plants, so both sexes are needed for berries. Reliable choices include 'Nymans' ♀, female, and 'Rubella' ♀, male, with red winter flower buds. Height 1m (3ft), spread 2m (6ft). It is a tough shrub for both borders and woodland gardens. Grow in either partial or full shade.
◫ – ☀ ◊ ❋ ❋ ❋

Symphoricarpos × chenaultii 'Hancock'
This is a spreading, mound-forming, deciduous shrub which makes useful, dense ground cover in any situation. White flowers are followed by small, sparsely produced, deep pink berries. Height 1m (3ft), spread 1.5m (5ft). Grow in full sun or partial shade. It tolerates poor soil, pollution, and exposure to cold winds.
▨ – ◧ ◊ ❋ ❋ ❋

VIBURNUM CARLESII

Viburnum
A large and diverse group of deciduous and evergreen shrubs that provide colour and interest for all seasons in shrub or mixed borders and woodland gardens. Among the best is the deciduous V. carlesii and 'Aurora' ♀, which produce fragrant, white and pink flowers, respectively, in spring; height and spread 2m (6ft). Grow in any soil, in full sun or partial shade.
▨ – ◧ ◊ ❋ ❋ ❋
V. opulus, see p.55

RHODODENDRONS AND AZALEAS

RHODODENDRON
YAKUSHIMANUM

Rhododendron
This is a huge group of evergreen and deciduous shrubs that includes azaleas. They make an impressive flower display, mainly in spring or early summer. Grow them in a moisture-retentive soil that is rich in humus, in a shrub border or woodland garden since they like dappled shade. All rhododendrons must be grown in an acid soil.
◧ ◊ ❋ ❋ ❋

R. 'Hinomayo' ♀
Evergreen hybrid azalea with pink flowers from mid-spring to early summer. Height and spread 60cm (24in).
R. luteum ♀
Deciduous azalea with fragrant, yellow flowers from late spring to early summer. Height and spread 4m (12ft).
R. yakushimanum hybrids
Compact evergreens with flowers in various colours and dark, glossy leaves. Height and spread up to 2m (6ft).

PERENNIALS

THESE FORM AN IMPORTANT GROUP of plants and, being non-woody, contrast well with shrubs in mixed borders. Many perennials are high-maintenance, needing staking, regular division, and sometimes frost protection, but the ones listed here are all fully hardy and self-supporting. Some, such as *Acanthus*, need to have their dead stems cut down annually, a relatively quick process.

FERNS

Athyrium filix-femina ♀
(Lady fern)
Herbaceous fern with pale green, erect fronds. Height 1.2m (4ft), spread to 90cm (36in). Grow in moist, neutral to acid soil in shade.
❃ ◊ ❀ ❀ ❀

Dryopteris filix-mas ♀
(Male fern)
Herbaceous fern with mid-green, upright fronds. Height and spread 90cm (36in). Grow in moist soil in a sheltered site.
◙ ◊ ❀ ❀ ❀

Polystichum aculeatum ♀
(Hard shield fern)
Evergreen fern with deep green, upright fronds, suitable for partial or full shade. Height 60cm (24in), spread 90cm (36in).
❃ – ◙ ◊ ❀ ❀ ❀

DRYOPTERIS FILIX-MAS

Acanthus spinosus ♀
(Bear's breeches)
This has long, deeply cut leaves with spiny edges and, in summer, tall stems of white flowers with purple bracts. Height 1.2m (4ft), spread 60–90cm (24–36in). Grow in deep soil, and cut down dead stems in autumn.
◨ – ◙ ◊ ❀ ❀ ❀

Ajuga reptans (Bugle)
A spreading, ground-hugging, evergreen perennial making superb flowering ground cover. Spires of deep blue flowers appear in late spring and early summer. Height 15cm (6in), spread 60–90cm (24–36in). Those forms with coloured foliage, such as 'Variegata' and dark purple 'Atropurpurea' ♀, are particularly effective.
◙ – ❃ ◊ ❀ ❀ ❀
A. reptans 'Catlin's Giant' ♀, *see p.28*

Alchemilla mollis ♀
(Lady's mantle)
This is a very good ground-cover plant for borders and woodland gardens. Pale green, lobed foliage provides an attractive backdrop for the frothy sprays of yellow-green summer flowers. Height 60cm (24in), spread 75cm (30in).
◨ – ◙ ◊ ❀ ❀ ❀
Also recommended: *A. mollis* 'Robusta'

Bergenia
Evergreen, spring-flowering perennials with large, rounded leaves that combine well with paving, sculpture, and shrubs. There are many to choose from, such as *B. cordifolia* with rose-red flowers. Moist soil in sun or partial shade is preferred, but they tolerate poor soil. Height to 60cm (24in), spread to 75cm (30in).
◨ – ◙ ◊ ❀ ❀ ❀
Bergenia, *see p.55*

Geranium (Cranesbill)
Summer-flowering, ground-cover perennials, ideal for borders or woodland gardens. There are many; try the bright pink, evergreen *G. endressii* ♀, height 45cm (18in), spread 60cm (24in). Cut off dead leaves in autumn.
◨ – ◙ ◊ ❀ ❀ ❀

GERANIUM ENDRESSII

HELLEBORUS ARGUTIFOLIUS

Helleborus (Hellebore)
Winter- or spring-flowering
evergreen perennials ideal for
a border or woodland garden.
Particularly recommended is
H. argutifolius ♥, with its
pale green flowers, height
1.2m (4ft), spread 90cm
(36in). Grow hellebores in
any humus-rich, moist soil.
🔲 ◊ ❋ ❋ ❋

Hemerocallis (Day lily)
These herbaceous perennials
with lily-like summer flowers
and attractive, broad, grassy
leaves are ideal for shrub or

mixed borders. They look as
good in modern settings as in
cottage gardens. Cut down
dead growth in autumn.
▣ ◊ ❋ ❋ ❋

Pachysandra terminalis ♥
Evergreen perennial grown for
its glossy, deep green foliage.
It makes fine, free-spreading
ground cover in full or partial
shade. Use among shrubs or
in a woodland garden. Height
20cm (8in), spread indefinite.
Any soil is suitable except
excessively dry conditions.
🔲 – ▣ ◊ ❋ ❋ ❋

Phormium
Evergreen plants with sword-
like foliage that looks right in
modern settings. Many have
striped leaves – for example,
P. cookianum subsp. *hookeri*
'Tricolor' ♥ has green, cream-
yellow, and red foliage.
▣ ◊ ❋ ❋

Pulmonaria (Lungwort)
Low-growing, herbaceous or
evergreen, spring-flowering,
ground-cover perennials for a
shrub border or woodland
garden. Try *P. angustifolia* ♥,

PULMONARIA ANGUSTIFOLIA
SUBSP. *AZUREA*

and subsp. *azurea* with rich
blue flowers; height 30cm
(12in), spread 45cm (18in).
🔲 – ▣ ◊ ❋ ❋ ❋

Stachys byzantina ♥
(Lamb's ears)
A mat-forming evergreen,
with grey-green leaves and
pink-purple flowers, that
makes excellent ground cover.
Height 45cm (18in), spread
60cm (24in). 'Big Ears' has
grey-white, felted, green
leaves, and 'Silver Carpet'
is non-flowering.
▣ – 🔲 ◊ ❋ ❋ ❋

SUBSTITUTES FOR A GRASS LAWN

In small areas, you can
create a more labour-saving
lawn with low-growing,
spreading, aromatic plants,
closely planted and regularly
trimmed to ensure dense
growth. Alternatively, grow
them in the cracks in paving.

Chamaemelum nobile
'Treneague'
A non-flowering chamomile.
▣ ◊ ❋ ❋ ❋

THYMUS SERPYLLUM

Mentha (Mint)
Use one of the procumbent
mints such as *M. pulegium*
(pennyroyal) or *M. requienii*
(Corsican mint).
▣ – 🔲 ◊ ❋ ❋ ❋

Thymus serpyllum
Use this creeping thyme or
one of its many cultivars,
such as 'Annie Hall' and
'Pink Chintz' ♥.
▣ ◊ ❋ ❋ ❋

GRASSES, BAMBOOS, AND SEDGES

THESE PLANTS HAVE A VARIETY of architectural forms and some are noted for their pleasing, feathery flowerheads. They can either be grouped together, or combined with shrubs and perennials in a border. Large ones can also be used as specimen plants. Cut down the herbaceous kinds in early spring.

Carex oshimensis 'Evergold' ♀

An evergreen, grass-like sedge with arching green and yellow striped leaves, and brown flower spikes in spring, ideal for planting by water features, paving, or pebbles. Height and spread 30cm (12in). Grow in sun or partial shade. ◐–◙ ◊ ❆❆❆

Fargesia murieliae ♀
(Umbrella bamboo)

A non-invasive bamboo with yellow arching canes (stems) and bright green, evergreen foliage. Height 4m (12ft), spread 1.5m (5ft) or more. It makes a fine specimen plant or focal point. This is a good choice for a container, and also suitable for a hedge or screen. It tolerates wind. Grow in sun or partial shade. ◐–◙ ◊ ❆❆❆

CAREX OSHIMENSIS 'EVERGOLD'

MISCANTHUS SINENSIS 'SILBERFEDER'

Festuca glauca (Blue fescue)

Evergreen grass with narrow, erect, blue-green leaves. It is excellent for a gravel garden or paved area, or grown in bold groups in a shrub or mixed border. Height and spread 30cm (12in). It will tolerate a poor, dry soil. ◐ ◊ ❆❆❆

F. glauca, see p.12; F. glauca 'Elijah Blue', see p.35

Hakonechloa macra 'Aureola' ♀

Herbaceous grass with arching, bright yellow and green striped leaves, providing a bright splash of colour in a border or woodland garden. It is ideal for patio containers. Height 35cm (14in), spread 40cm (16in). It will grow in sun, but the best colour is achieved in partial shade. ◐–◙ ◊ ❆❆❆

Miscanthus sinensis ♀

Herbaceous grass with blue-green leaves and feathery heads of silky, purple-tinted flowers. Height 4m (12ft), spread 1.2m (4ft). 'Silberfeder' has silvery to pale pinkish-brown flowers, height 2.5m (8ft); 'Variegatus' has leaves longitudinally banded white and green, height 1.8m (6ft). ◐ ◊ ❆❆❆

Phyllostachys nigra ♀
(Black bamboo)

A bamboo with deep green foliage, whose arching green canes eventually turn black. Height 3–5m (10–15ft), spread 2–3m (6–10ft). This is a good specimen plant for modern settings, especially near paving or pebbles, and is suitable for patio containers. ◐–◙ ◊ ❆❆❆

P. nigra ♀, see p.35

PHYLLOSTACHYS NIGRA

BULBOUS PLANTS

THE MOST LABOUR-SAVING WAY to grow many bulbous plants is to allow them to become 'naturalized' – which means leaving them to spread and increase naturally. Grow them in bold, informal drifts or groups among shrubs or in areas of grass. Feed them after flowering, and remove the dead leaves.

CHIONODOXA FORBESII

Chionodoxa forbesii
(Glory of the snow)
This very popular small bulb produces star-shaped, blue, white-centred flowers in early spring. Height 15cm (6in), spread 3cm (1¼in). It is ideal for growing under shrubs and trees and in grass. It self-seeds freely and therefore soon spreads into a large colony. Easily grown, it is suited to any well-drained soil.
◩ ◊ ✿ ✿ ✿

Crocus
There are both spring- and autumn-flowering crocuses, all ideal for naturalizing in grass or borders. One of the best spring-flowering species is C. tommasinianus ♥, which has lilac to purple flowers; height 8–10cm (3–4in), spread 2.5cm (1in). C. vernus (Dutch crocus), bears lilac, purple, or white flowers in spring; height

10–12cm (4–5in), spread 5cm (2in). The autumn-flowering C. speciosus ♥ has violet-blue flowers and self-seeds freely; height 10–15cm (4–6in), spread 5cm (2in).
◩ ◊ ✿ ✿ ✿

Galanthus (Snowdrop)
Most snowdrops, and there are many to choose from, have white flowers with green markings. All of them are ideal for naturalizing in grass, woodland, or shrub borders. Recommended plants include: G. 'Atkinsii' ♥, flowering in late winter, height 20cm (8in), spread 8cm (3in); G. nivalis ♥ (Common snowdrop), winter-flowering, height and spread 10cm (4in); and G. nivalis 'Flore Pleno' ♥, with double flowers. Grow in partial shade in a moist, humus-rich soil.
◪ ◊ ✿ ✿ ✿

GALANTHUS 'ATKINSII'

MUSCARI ARMENIACUM

Muscari armeniacum ♥
This grape hyacinth produces long-lasting, fat, stumpy spikes of bright blue flowers in spring. Spreading freely from seeds and bulblets, it is ideal for naturalizing in grass and shrub borders. Height 20cm (8in), spread 5cm (2in). It is suited to any moisture-retentive soil.
◩ ◊ ✿ ✿ ✿

Narcissus (Daffodil)
Some of the miniature species, such as N. bulbocodium ♥ (Hoop-petticoat daffodil), are ideal for naturalizing in grass, shrub borders, and woodland gardens, as are the larger Narcissus hybrids, such as Trumpet daffodils. Different colours are available. Grow in any moist soil (neutral to acid for N. bulbocodium) in full sun or partial shade.
◩ – ◪ ◊ ✿ ✿ ✿

INDEX

Page numbers in *bold italics* indicate illustrations.

ACKNOWLEDGMENTS

Picture research Amanda Russell
Picture librarian Richard Dabb
Special photography Peter Anderson
Illustrations Karen Gavin, Gill Tomblin
Index Hilary Bird

Dorling Kindersley would like to thank:
Alan Toogood for modelling, Hillier Garden
Centres for the loan of props, and all staff at
the RHS, in particular Susanne Mitchell, Karen
Wilson and Barbara Haynes at Vincent Square.

Photography
The publisher would also like to thank the
following for their kind permission to
reproduce their photographs:
(key: t=top, c=centre, b=below, l=left, r=right)

Peter Anderson: 51c.
Garden Picture Library: Brigitte Thomas 16br;
Christi Carter 31t; Christopher Gallaher 36;
Clive Nichols 49b; David Askham 39tl; Geoff
Ban 53b; Howard Rice 21t, John Baker 18br;
John Glover 7, 20b; JS Sira 33t, 14b, 47br;
Lamontagne 38; Marianne Majerus 43; Neil

Holmes 22b; Ron Evans 42; Ron Sutherland 2,
8b, 15t, 25t, 42, 45br; Steven Wooster 53t.
John Glover: 16l, 28b, 47c, 47bl, 51b, 66.
Andrew Lawson: 12br, 33c, 39cr.
Clive Nichols: 6, 19t; Beth Chatto Garden,
Essex 23t; Design Vic Shanley 34; Lakemount,
Cork, Eire 40; Sue Berger 27t; The Old
Vicarage, Norfolk 41.
Steven Wooster: Robin Templar Williams
design 9.

Cover photography: **Peter Anderson** back
cover tr; **Garden Picture Library**, Christopher
Gallaher front cover bl; John Glover front cover
tcl; **John Glover** front cover tl, back cover b.

The Royal Horticultural Society
To learn more about the work of the Society,
visit the RHS on the internet at **www.rhs.
org.uk**. Information offered includes plant
news, horticultural events around the country,
RHS *Plant Finder*, a garden finder, inter-
national plant registers, results of plant trials,
a gardening calendar and monthly topics of
interest, publications, and membership details.